Elements of Literature

Fourth Course

HOLT ASSESSMENT
Writing, Listening, and Speaking
Tests and Answer Key

- ■ **Workshop Tests in Standardized Test Formats**
- ■ **Evaluation Forms**
- ■ **Scales and Rubrics**
- ■ **Holistic Scoring Guides**
- ■ **6 Traits—Plus 1 Analytical Scale**
- ■ **Sample Papers**
- ■ **Portfolio Assessment**

HOLT, RINEHART AND WINSTON

A Harcourt Education Company

Orlando • **Austin** • New York • San Diego • Toronto • London

STAFF CREDITS

EDITORIAL

Executive Editor
Kristine E. Marshall

Senior Editor
Julie Barnett Hoover

Project Editor
Jane Kominek

Copyediting
Michael Neibergall, *Copyediting Manager;* Mary Malone, *Copyediting Supervisor;* Christine Altgelt, Elizabeth Dickson, *Senior Copyeditors;* Emily Force, Julia Thomas Hu, *Copyeditors*

Project Administration
Marie Price, *Managing Editor;* Betty Gabriel, *Project Administration*

Editorial Permissions
Ann B. Farrar, *Senior Permissions Editor*

ART, DESIGN, AND PHOTO

Graphic Services
Kristen Darby, *Manager*

Cover Design
Dick Metzger, *Design Director;* Sunday Patterson, *Designer*

PRODUCTION

Belinda Barbosa Lopez, Michael Roche, *Senior Production Coordinators*
Carol Trammel, *Production Supervisor*
Beth Prevelige, *Senior Production Manager*

MANUFACTURING/ INVENTORY

Shirley Cantrell, *Manufacturing Supervisor*
Amy Borseth, *Manufacturing Coordinator*
Mark McDonald, *Inventory Planner*

Printed in the United States of America

ISBN 0-03-068513-3

1 2 3 4 5 6   179   07 06 05 04 03

Table of Contents

Overview of ELEMENTS OF LITERATURE Assessment Program

Writing Workshop Tests and Answer Key

for Student Edition
pp. 56–939

Multiple-choice test for
each Writing Workshop

Table of Contents *continued*

Workshop Scales and Rubrics

Table of Contents *continued*

Scales and Sample Papers

Portfolio Assessment

Table of Contents *continued*

Overview of ELEMENTS OF LITERATURE Assessment Program

Two assessment booklets have been developed for ELEMENTS OF LITERATURE.

(1) Assessment of student mastery of selections and specific literary, reading, and vocabulary skills in the **Student Edition:**

- *Holt Assessment: Literature, Reading, and Vocabulary*

(2) Assessment of student mastery of workshops and specific writing, listening, and speaking skills in the **Student Edition:**

- *Holt Assessment: Writing, Listening, and Speaking*

Diagnostic Assessment

Holt Assessment: Literature, Reading, and Vocabulary contains two types of diagnostic tests:

- The Entry-Level Test is a diagnostic tool that helps you determine (1) how well students have mastered essential prerequisite skills needed for the year and (2) to what degree students understand the concepts that will be taught during the current year. This test uses multiple tasks to assess mastery of literary, reading, and vocabulary skills.

- The Collection Diagnostic Tests help you determine the extent of students' prior knowledge of literary, reading, and vocabulary skills taught in each collection. These tests provide vital information that will assist you in helping students master collection skills.

Holt Online Essay Scoring can be used as a diagnostic tool to evaluate students' writing proficiency:

- For each essay, the online scoring system delivers a holistic score and analytic feedback related to five writing traits. These two scoring methods will enable you to pinpoint the strengths of your students' writing as well as skills that need improvement.

Ongoing, Informal Assessment

The **Student Edition** offers systematic opportunities for ongoing, informal assessment and immediate instructional follow-up. Students' responses to their reading; their writing, listening, and speaking projects; and their work with vocabulary skills all serve as both instructional and ongoing assessment tasks.

Overview of ELEMENTS OF LITERATURE
Assessment Program *continued*

- Throughout the **Student Edition,** practice and assessment are immediate and occur at the point where skills are taught.

- In order for assessment to inform instruction on an on-going basis, related material repeats instruction and then offers new opportunities for informal assessment.

- **Skills Reviews** at the end of each collection offer a quick evaluation of how well students have mastered the collection skills.

Progress Assessment

Students' mastery of the content of the **Student Edition** is systematically assessed in two test booklets:

- *Holt Assessment: Literature, Reading, and Vocabulary* offers a test for every selection. Multiple-choice questions focus on comprehension, the selected skills, and vocabulary development. In addition, students write answers to constructed-response prompts that test their understanding of the skills.

- *Holt Assessment: Writing, Listening, and Speaking* provides both multiple-choice questions for writing and analytical scales and rubrics for writing, listening, and speaking. These instruments assess proficiency in all the writing applications appropriate for each grade level.

Summative Assessment

Holt Assessment: Literature, Reading, and Vocabulary contains two types of summative tests:

- The Collection Summative Tests, which appear at the end of every collection, ask students to apply their recently acquired skills to a new literary selection. These tests contain both multiple-choice questions and constructed-response prompts.

- The End-of-Year Test helps you determine how well students have mastered the skills and concepts taught during the year. This test mirrors the Entry-Level Test and uses multiple tasks to assess mastery of literary, reading, and vocabulary skills.

Overview of Elements of Literature
Assessment Program *continued*

Holt Online Essay Scoring can be used as an end-of-year assessment tool:

- You can use *Holt Online Essay Scoring* to evaluate how well students have mastered the writing skills taught during the year. You will be able to assess student mastery using a holistic score as well as analytic feedback based on five writing traits.

Monitoring Student Progress

Both *Holt Assessment: Literature, Reading, and Vocabulary* and *Holt Assessment: Writing, Listening, and Speaking* include skills profiles that record progress toward the mastery of skills. Students and teachers can use the profiles to monitor student progress.

One-Stop Planner® CD-ROM with ExamView® Test Generator

All of the questions in this booklet are available on the *One-Stop Planner*® **CD-ROM with ExamView® Test Generator.** You can use the ExamView Test Generator to customize any of the tests in this booklet. You can then print a test unique to your classroom situation.

Holt Online Assessment

You can use *Holt Online Assessment* to administer and score the diagnostic and summative tests online. You can then generate and print reports to document student growth and class results. For your students, this online resource provides individual assessment of strengths and weaknesses and immediate feedback.

About This Book

This book, *Holt Assessment: Writing, Listening, and Speaking,* accompanies the ELEMENTS OF LITERATURE program and provides a variety of assessment resources. These include Writing Workshop Tests and Answer Key, Workshop Scales and Rubrics, Scales and Sample Papers, and Portfolio Assessment.

WRITING WORKSHOP TESTS AND ANSWER KEY

Every Writing Workshop in ELEMENTS OF LITERATURE has an accompanying Writing Workshop Test in a standardized test format. The test format not only will allow you to assess student performance but also will familiarize students with standardized tests and give them experience in test taking.

Each Writing Workshop Test provides a passage containing problems or errors in several or all of the following areas: content, organization, style, and conventions. Students demonstrate their understanding of the writing genre and their revising and proofreading skills by responding to multiple-choice items. Students revise elements of the genre, restructure segments of the passage, add or delete statements, refine language, and correct errors in the passage.

Answer Sheets

Answer Sheets immediately follow the tests in this section. The Answer Sheets correspond to the answer options on a particular standardized test. Use the following chart to help you determine which answer sheet to use.

Workshop	Answer Sheet
Writing Workshops for Collections 1–8 and 10–11	Answer Sheet 1
Writing Workshop for Collection 9	Answer Sheet 2

Answer Key

The Answer Key follows the Answer Sheets at the end of this section of the book. In addition to giving the correct answer, the Answer Key tells which Workshop skill is assessed by each item.

About This Book *continued*

WORKSHOP SCALES AND RUBRICS

This section contains analytical scales and scoring rubrics for Writing Workshops and scales for Listening and Speaking Workshops. Both the scales and the rubrics are important teacher evaluation tools. In addition, students can use scales and rubrics as learning and evaluation guides for their own work.

The **scales** include essential criteria for mastery of skills and ratings of each criterion based on a four-point scale. The **rubrics** are based on the same criteria listed in the scales. The rubrics clearly describe a student's work at each score point level for each specific criterion.

Score Point 0

On occasion, student work may be unscorable and consequently will receive a score point of zero. This may be true of writing, listening and speaking, and media assignments. The following are reasons to give a product a score of zero. The work

- is not relevant to the prompt or assignment
- is only a rewording of the prompt or assignment
- contains an insufficient amount of writing (or other mode) to determine whether it addresses the prompt or assignment
- is a copy of previously published work
- is illegible, incomprehensible, blank, or in a language other than English

About This Book *continued*

SCALES AND SAMPLE PAPERS

This section contains two different kinds of scales for assessing writing: The 6 Traits—Plus 1 Analytical Scale and the individual four-point holistic scales for biographical or autobiographical writing, exposition, responses to literature, persuasion, and business letters. Accompanying these scales are high-level, mid-level, and low-level examples of student writing. Individual evaluations, based on the analytical and holistic scales, follow each sample student paper. These scales can be used for on-demand writing or class assignments. Although this section is directed to teachers, students may also benefit from access to this section as they write and revise.

PORTFOLIO ASSESSMENT

This section provides an introduction to portfolio work, including suggestions about how to develop and use portfolios and how to conduct conferences with students about their work.

Forms

The introductory article is followed by a set of student forms for assessing and organizing portfolio contents and for setting goals for future work. Also included is a set of forms for communicating with parents or guardians about student work and for generally assessing students' progress.

Forms in this section can be used to record work, to establish baselines and goals, and to think critically about student work in a variety of areas. These areas include writing, listening, and speaking. The goal of these forms is to encourage students to develop criteria for assessing their own work and to identify areas for improvement. Many forms can also be used for assessment of a peer's work and for teacher evaluations.

Writing Workshop Tests and Answer Key

for **COLLECTION 1** | page 56

Writing Workshop: Autobiographical Narrative

DIRECTIONS The following is a draft of an autobiographical narrative about a student's decision to major in biology. It contains errors in development and organization. Some of the questions refer to underlined words or phrases or to numbered sentences within the text. Read the essay and answer questions 1 through 10.

What's in a Name?

I have always liked birds. As a child, I kept a log in which I described in
(1)   (2)
loopy handwriting the sight of a soaring red-tailed hawk and the <u>pleasant</u>

song of the western meadowlark. I decided to specialize in birds as a
(3)
career. However, when my first serious science textbook was not full of
(4)
glossy pictures of beautiful birds, reality hit me. I halfheartedly learned
(5)
that one magnificent bird of prey is called *Buteo jamaicensis*, and the fluting

trill that woke me on summer mornings belongs to the *Sturnella neglecta*.

I almost closed the book on birds.
(6)
When I complained that the scientific names were boring and confusing,
(7)
my teacher explained that scientific naming is simple and logical. She
(8)
asked me to prepare a short report on the guidelines for naming new

species. I was surprised and intrigued when I learned how to break the
(9)
code of the names. In order to share information and prevent confusion,
(10)
scientists from around the world use a universal method of identifying

animals. Once names are assigned, they can never be changed by individu-
(11)
als. After learning the logic behind the naming process, I felt more
(12)
comfortable with the scientific names.

After I gave my report on the guidelines for scientific naming, my friend
(13)
Andrew remarked, "Aren't these names a lot like human names? Each
(14)
animal has a first, middle, and last name, as well as nicknames." I realized
(15)
that he was right. In addition, I saw that the scientific names often provide
(16)
clues to birth dates, locations, and relatives. Suddenly, the world of
(17)

GO ON ➤

scientific naming became even clearer than before. Of course, some people
(18)
have more than three names, while others have only two. What had
(19)
seemed like an impenetrable maze of scientific jargon was, in fact, simply
a puzzle that was easily deciphered once I knew the key.

Most important, though, for changing my attitude—and my life—was
(20)
learning that scientific names are creative and fun. They often demonstrate
(21)
a sense of humor and history. Geography is covered, too. Several days
(22)   (23)
after my report, I was idly flipping through my textbook when my eye was
caught by several names that I remembered from literature classes. For
(24)
example, the *Antheraea polyphemus* moth is named for a character in the
Odyssey, while a *Zeus* is a powerful fish, and the *Draculoides bramstokeri* is
a spider. I was amused by *Agra vation*, a beetle, and *Verae peculya*, a wasp.
(25)
The *Panama canalia* and the *Australia* are both wasps. The people who
(26)   (27)
named these creatures managed to provide unique, descriptive names.

From *A* (*Aaadonta*, a snail) to *Z* (*Zyzzyzus*, a hydroid, plantlike sea
(28)
creature), puns and other forms of wordplay are used to name creatures.

With this in mind, I approached my ornithology textbook with renewed
(29)
interest. I could see a wealth of knowledge in the lists of names, which
(30)
were open before me. Now I look forward to spending my days teaching
(31)
young people about the stories behind the names of science.

1 What would be the BEST replacement
for sentence 1?

A   more background information

B   a more attention-getting sentence

C   a strong opinion

D   a description of the narrator

2 What is the MOST specific modifier to
replace <u>pleasant</u> in sentence 2?

A   nice

B   musical

C   flutelike

D   pretty

GO ON

3 **What background information should be added after sentence 4?**

A   Instead, the textbook had long lists of unfamiliar, scientific names.

B   I have always enjoyed looking at beautiful photographs of birds.

C   Without pictures, the textbook was boring.

D   Beautifully colored birds catch anyone's eye.

4 **What sentence should be added after sentence 6?**

A   I am glad that I didn't, because I have learned a lot since then.

B   However, I love birds too much to give up studying them.

C   You can learn interesting things by studying the names of birds.

D   Then I realized that fascinating stories are hidden in these names.

5 **What factual detail would BEST be added after sentence 10?**

A   Many people do not know the logic behind scientific names.

B   Some names reveal where an animal lives or where it was first identified.

C   Each name must uniquely identify the animal.

D   Some scientists might not have wanted to follow the guidelines.

6 **Which sentence should be deleted to remove irrelevant information?**

A   18

B   19

C   21

D   23

7 **Which sentence should be moved to precede sentence 26?**

A   20

B   22

C   24

D   27

8 **What should be added to the end of sentence 27 to include the writer's thoughts?**

A   that indicate something about the named creatures

B   and to help preserve a logical system of naming life-forms

C   and to make biology students smile for years to come

D   that help scientists classify these creatures

9 **How should** were open before me **in sentence 30 BEST be written to add figurative language?**

A   were open before me like a book I looked forward to reading

B   opened before me like an umbrella that would give me knowledge

C   were spread out before me

D   were open before me like an ancient scroll full of intriguing tales

10 **Which sentence should be added after sentence 30 to state the significance of the experience?**

A   I enjoyed studying the lists of names and learning the secrets they carried.

B   Deciphering their meaning inspired me to be a biology teacher.

C   Studying the lists helped me make good grades in my biology classes.

D   The lists of names included information about many subjects.

for **COLLECTION 2**   *page 122*

Writing Workshop: Biographical Narrative

DIRECTIONS The following is a rough draft of a biographical narrative about a student's grandfather. It contains errors in development and organization. Questions refer to underlined words or numbered sentences within the text. Read the narrative and answer questions 1 through 10.

The Coverup

I'll never forget when I realized there was more to my grandfather than
(1)
his hard-nosed look and rough exterior. To me, Pa-Paw was a giant with a
(2)
deep, baritone voice and a square, intimidating jaw.

He sat in his favorite chair while the radio next to him blasted country-
(3)
and-western music. With his blue eyes closed and his gray eyebrows
(4)
drawn together, Pa-Paw looked ferocious. The changes in Pa-Paw made me
(5)
feel as if I were watching a metamorphosis. Then the sad song ended, and
(6)
a lively tune began. His eyebrows eased up. He smiled and seemed happy.
(7)   (8)
His head came off the back of the chair, and his eyes opened and actually
(9)
twinkled at me! At that moment, Pa-Paw became a real person to me.
(10)

The next day, he surprised me again by asking me to go on his daily
(11)
walk with him. I was a little nervous but agreed. As we passed under
(12)   (13)
century-old oaks that lined the sidewalk, we didn't speak. Then Pa-Paw
(14)
began to whistle. That lilting sound reminded me of something I'd long
(15)
forgotten.

That night, Pa-Paw didn't turn on the radio. Instead, he went into his
(16)   (17)
bedroom and came out with a fiddle in one hand and a bow in the other.

Without saying a word, he walked stoically out the front door. I looked at
(18)   (19)
Ma-Maw. The wide grin on her face was enough to make me hop up like
(20)
a jack rabbit and run out onto the darkened porch. Within minutes, Pa-Paw
(21)
had the fiddle tucked under his no-longer-intimidating jaw and was play-

ing a toe-tapping reel. Seeing him so happy, so filled with that music, made
(22)
me realize he wasn't such a hard man after all.

> That's when I started noticing other things—things I'd seen Pa-Paw do
> (23)
> a hundred times before but never thought too much about. For example,
> (24)
> many times I had watched him feed stray cats. Every night, he'd go out the
> (25)
> back door and pour cat food into four or five bowls. I usually paid more
> (26)
> attention to the cats, but one night that summer I watched Pa-Paw, too.
>
> "They're cute," I said as he squatted down to pour the food, his broad
> (27)
> back <u>very</u> straight.
>
> "They're hungry," Pa-Paw said, his gruff look back in place.
> (28)
> "I think it's nice you feed them," I persisted.
> (29)
> Pa-Paw stood back up, turned, and gave me that hard-nosed look I
> (30)
> was so familiar with, but there was something else in that look, as well.
>
> I smiled. Pa-Paw smiled back.
> (31)   (32)

1 **What background information should be added after sentence 1?**

A   It is a long story, but I'll summarize.

B   Since then, I have seen photographs of him as a young man.

C   We do not always know our own relatives as well as we think we do.

D   I was about twelve years old when I visited him that summer.

2 **Which sentence, if added after sentence 2, BEST hints at the significance of the subject?**

A   Pa-Paw must have been in his sixties then, but to me he seemed much older.

B   Later, I would learn that Pa-Paw had actually worked as a paid fiddler.

C   I had always felt comfortable in Pa-Paw's house, which seemed like a refuge from the cares of the world.

D   Because Pa-Paw did not talk much, I had never felt that I knew him, but that was about to change.

3 **What details should precede sentence 3 to make the setting clear?**

A   One night, something drew me to the living room, where I saw a side of Pa-Paw I had never seen before.

B   Pa-Paw liked to listen to music, I learned to my surprise.

C   Pa-Paw fed stray cats in the neighborhood, and I had always wanted to take one of the cats home with me.

D   I had not known that Pa-Paw was an accomplished fiddler.

4 **To preserve chronological order, sentence 6 should be moved to follow which sentence?**

A   3
B   4
C   7
D   9

GO ON

5 **What is the BEST revision of sentence 8?**

A   He tapped his feet and smiled happi-
     ly as he listened to the music.

B   It was obvious that he was happy,
     because he was smiling as he listened
     to the music.

C   His big feet began tapping on the
     carpet, and his mouth lifted into a
     wide, happy smile.

D   He smiled and tapped his feet as he
     listened to the music being broadcast
     over the radio.

6 **Which sentence would BEST follow
sentence 15?**

A   This event occurred outside on the
     sidewalk in front of Pa-Paw's house.

B   "Do you still play the fiddle,
     Pa-Paw?" I asked, but his mumbled
     reply was noncommittal.

C   I like to hear Pa-Paw whistle old
     tunes that seem to cheer him up.

D   It was early morning, and birds
     were chirping their songs, too, as
     though they were singing along
     with Pa-Paw.

7 **Which sentence should be added after
sentence 22 to BEST reveal the writer's
thoughts and feelings?**

A   Now he plays his fiddle more often.

B   Since then, he has told me that play-
     ing the fiddle makes him happy.

C   The neighbors came outside to listen
     to him play.

D   Maybe his tough exterior was just a
     coverup.

8 **What word would BEST replace very in
sentence 27?**

A   really

B   somewhat

C   rigidly

D   so

9 **Which sentence should be added after
sentence 30?**

A   I wasn't sure what it was, but I
     thought it was good.

B   From the light on the back porch,
     I saw the twinkle in Pa-Paw's eyes.

C   Maybe someday I would understand
     my grandfather better.

D   I thought of his fiddle playing and
     what Ma-Maw had told me.

10 **Which sentence should be added to the
end of the narrative?**

A   He had shown me that actions may
     reveal more about character than
     words do.

B   I am glad that I spent that vacation
     time with my grandfather.

C   I think he was pleased that I had
     come for a visit.

D   After that experience, I wanted to
     spend every holiday and vacation
     with Pa-Paw and his cats.

Writing Workshop: Analyzing Problems and Solutions

DIRECTIONS The following is a rough draft of an essay analyzing the problem of a shortage of volunteers for charitable work and presenting a solution to the problem. The essay contains errors in organization and development. Some of the questions refer to underlined words or numbered sentences in the essay. Read the essay and answer questions 1 through 10.

Time to Help

Most of us are totally caught up in our own lives. We never seem to
(1)   (2)
have enough time for everything we want to do. We have to do homework
(3)
and help with household tasks. However, we usually do have some free
(4)
time on weekends, during school breaks, and in the summer. What are we
(5)
doing with that free time? Are we giving back to our community? Are we
(6)   (7)
helping others? Many organizations suffer from a lack of volunteers, but
(8)
we teenagers can find the time to use our skills to help these organizations.

The problem of lack of volunteers has increased in recent years as more
(9)
people work longer hours and face increasing demands on their time.

Organizations that rely on volunteers often have to cut services to people
(10)
who have pressing needs. While the number of people who need support
(11)
and assistance continues to increase, the number of people who perform

volunteer services has not kept up with the need.

To help solve the problem of a shortage of volunteer workers, some
(12)
people have proposed requiring community service for graduation from

high school. Some school districts have already introduced this require-
(13)
ment, but mandatory community service is a hardship for some students.

Some teenagers must work to help support their families or to earn money
(14)
for college.

Teens can best address the problem of finding the time to volunteer for
(15)
hard-pressed service organizations by working with a school volunteer

GO ON

coordinator. The volunteer coordinator at your school can guide you to an
(16)
organization that needs your skills, and you might be surprised to learn

how many of your skills are needed. You don't need to be an honor student
(17)
to tutor a child. The school volunteer coordinator can also help you <u>lend a</u>
(18)
<u>helping hand to people</u> in need while retaining control of your schedules.

If you donate only an hour of your time each week, you will perform
(19)
fifty-two hours of charitable work in a year. The volunteer coordinator can
(20)
help teens match their tight schedules with the schedules of organizations

needing help.

    The problem of inadequate numbers of volunteers is a serious one, but
(21)
it can be alleviated. With the assistance of the school volunteer coordinator,
(22)
teens can find the time and skills to volunteer for organizations that have

a shortage of volunteers.

1 **Which sentence, if added to the beginning of the essay, would BEST grab the reader's attention?**

  A Everyone should give up some free time to perform volunteer work.

  B Helping charitable organizations can provide useful experience.

  C Are we sending a "too busy" message to those who need our help?

  D Most of us are very busy with homework and after-school activities.

2 **What background information should be added after sentence 2?**

  A Our parents and guardians are busy, too, but they usually take time to help us.

  B Maybe we try to fit too many activities into our week.

  C Some of us wish that a day had more than twenty-four hours.

  D We spend six to eight hours of each weekday in school.

3 **Which clause should be added to the end of sentence 8 to create a complete thesis statement?**

  A if we work with the school volunteer coordinator

  B but many of us are very busy nearly all the time

  C because even my younger sister helps every month

  D Leave as is.

GO ON

4 **What additional evidence would BEST be added after sentence 14?**

A   Students need to schedule volunteer work.

B   Others care for brothers or sisters, or even ill parents.

C   Students need fewer, not more, demands on their time.

D   Required community service is a good idea.

5 **Which sentence should follow sentence 17 to provide a specific example?**

A   We find time to do what we want to do almost every day.

B   Some honor students tutor young children.

C   You can teach a child a subject you have already mastered.

D   You can tutor many children who are younger than you.

6 **What is the BEST way to write** lend a helping hand to people **in sentence 18 to replace a cliché?**

A   be there for people

B   give of ourselves to people

C   provide valuable assistance to people

D   Leave as is.

7 **Which sentence would BEST follow sentence 20 to provide an example?**

A   My cousin discovered that he could serve dinner at the senior center right after band practice.

B   We should not think that we are too busy to help others.

C   Many organizations and individuals need our time and skills.

D   Some organizations give presentations to school groups to encourage teenagers to volunteer.

8 **What should be added to the end of sentence 21 to describe the BEST solution?**

A   when teenagers have time to work

B   most of the time by mandating community volunteer work

C   by the joint effort of teens and the school volunteer coordinator

D   Leave as is.

9 **Which call to action would BEST be added after sentence 22?**

A   Check your calendar to see when you can perform volunteer work.

B   Plan your vacation and holidays around a volunteer work schedule.

C   For what organization are you going to volunteer to work?

D   See your volunteer coordinator right away to schedule time to volunteer.

10 **Which emotional appeal would BEST be added to the end of the essay?**

A   While performing volunteer work, you often meet interesting people who share your interests.

B   Helping others is a duty that you should not avoid simply to spend time having fun.

C   If you want to make a difference in someone's life, share your time and skills with someone who urgently needs your help.

D   Community work you perform as a teenage volunteer can help prepare you to lead others when you get older.

for **COLLECTION 4**   *page 294*

Writing Workshop: Persuasive Essay

DIRECTIONS The following is a rough draft of a persuasive essay requesting more high school courses that introduce students to career options. It contains errors in sentence structure, organization, and development. Some of the questions refer to numbered sentences in the essay. Read the essay and answer questions 1 through 10.

Increase Our Options

Teenagers need to think about the future. Some career information is
(1)   (2)
missing from our education. We need information about other careers.
(3)

Competition for jobs is tough, and a college degree does not guarantee
(4)
a well-paid job. When I stopped at the nursery to buy some houseplants
(5)
yesterday, I talked with the employee watering the plants. He completed a
(6)
Ph.D. in mechanical engineering last May, but he is earning little more than

minimum wage while he continues to look for a job in his field. He is not
(7)
the only well-educated individual in such a situation.

Most important, though, is the fact that some stable, well-paid careers
(8)
are not taught in university courses. Mr. Henderson, an electrician who
(9)
lives across the street from me, usually earns more than $100,000 a year.

Even when new construction business is slow, Mr. Henderson finds work
(10)
rewiring older homes and office buildings. Many people will scrape togeth-
(11)
er the money to pay for electrical or car repairs even when doing so means

they must do without entertainment or cultural activities for a while. The
(12)
failure to provide introductory courses in auto repair, electrical work, and

plumbing makes it more difficult for students to learn about these career

options. My brother Andre likes to build and repair electronic devices such
(13)
as TV sets, radios, stereos, and VCRs. He is more interested in working
(14)
with the actual parts and wiring than in studying in a classroom.

Some people have skills and talents that are not developed in traditional
(15)
high school, college, or university courses. Taking apart and rebuilding
(16)

GO ON

transmissions is enjoyed by my friend Susan. Her father owns the auto
(17)
repair shop down the street from our school, and Susan has helped in

his shop for the past five years. Her father started out teaching her how
(18)
to change oil and spark plugs, and she enjoyed the work so much that

she asked him to teach her how to repair transmissions.

    Not everyone has a parent who can train him or her to repair transmis-
(19)
sions. Some students do not have access to electronic devices they can
(20)
use to teach themselves to build or repair the devices. Let's add courses
(21)
in every possible field, even if the course helps only one student.

1 **How should sentence 1 be written to grab the reader's attention?**

A Information about career options is important for teenagers.

B Some people might want to become plumbers or electricians instead of university professors.

C Shouldn't students have information about as many well-paid careers as possible?

D Studying in college is important, and so is learning about life.

2 **What background information should be added after sentence 2?**

A Some students wait until they start college to consider their career choices.

B Our counselors and teachers seem to focus on careers that require a college degree.

C Some universities and colleges specialize in certain fields.

D Deciding on a college can be difficult even when you have lots of information.

3 **What, if anything, should be added to the end of sentence 3 to create a clear opinion statement?**

A including those that require on-the-job training

B such as those in sports and entertainment

C that are not boring and poorly paid

D Leave as is.

4 **Which example should be added after sentence 7?**

A My neighbor is still looking for a job six months after she was laid off from her job developing software.

B He and I discussed the different kinds of houseplants that thrive in this climate.

C An advanced college degree does not necessarily help you find a well-paid, long-term job.

D People with college degrees sometimes find it hard to get and keep a well-paid job.

GO ON

5 Which group of sentences should be moved to the fourth paragraph to support the reason discussed in that paragraph?

A   5–6
B   8–10
C   13–14
D   20–21

6 Which paragraph should be moved to follow the fourth paragraph to organize the reasons from least important to most important?

A   first
B   second
C   third
D   Leave as is.

7 How should sentence 16 be written?

A   Taking apart transmissions is enjoyed by my friend Susan, who then rebuilds them.
B   My friend Susan enjoys taking apart and then rebuilding transmissions.
C   To take apart transmissions and then to rebuild them is enjoyed by my friend Susan.
D   Leave as is.

8 Which evidence should be added following sentence 18 to support the reason discussed in the fourth paragraph?

A   She also plans to obtain a computer science degree to prepare for working on computerized engines.
B   A college degree will help her keep her career options open.
C   She wants to open her own auto repair shop by the time she is thirty.
D   Susan often finds it difficult to learn in a classroom, but she learns quickly as she works.

9 Which restatement of the opinion should be added following sentence 20?

A   Electrical engineering courses at the university do not teach the skills that Andre has learned on his own.
B   We need introductory courses about careers that require on-the-job training.
C   Everyone needs to know how auto repairs are performed.
D   Such training can help students understand the problems encountered by people using equipment.

10 How should sentence 21 be written to provide an effective call to action?

A   Let's help students get degrees at good universities and colleges so that they can have successful careers.
B   Encourage students to consider their career options before they decide on a college or university.
C   Take a variety of courses so that you can decide what careers might interest you.
D   Let's work together to provide courses that introduce all students to more career options.

for **COLLECTION 5**   page 382

Writing Workshop: Comparing Media Genres

DIRECTIONS The following is a rough draft of an essay comparing how a magazine article and a Web site covered the discovery of crocodile fossils. It contains errors in development and organization. Some of the questions refer to underlined sections or numbered sentences within the text. Read the essay and answer questions 1 through 10.

Dinosaurs Are Mere Morsels

Recently discovered fossils of a crocodile named *Sarcosuchus imperator*
(1)
indicate that this cousin of the modern crocodile may have reached a length
of 40 feet and a weight of 18,000 pounds. It isn't every day that paleontolo-
(2)
gists find evidence of a creature that could treat 20-foot-long dinosaurs as
snacks. A comparison of a print magazine version of the story in *Science*
(3)
News (October 27, 2001) and a Web site presentation of the story reveals
differences in the treatments. The differences are related to the expected
(4)
audience and to the limitations of the media in which the story appears.

The magazine article's catchy title appeals to the reader, but the article
(5)
itself is a rather straightforward account of the find, with estimates of the
size of the creature. Vertebrate paleontologists are quoted as sources for
(6)
information about the fossil. The article includes only one photograph,
(7)
a picture of the fossil skull with the skull of a modern-day adult crocodile
shown inside it. The picture caption tells the reader the length of both
(8)
skulls. The article requires readers' sustained concentration but rewards
(9)
them with detailed information and sources.

In contrast, the Project Exploration Web site treats the story as entertain-
(10)
ment. The legend at the top of the Web page, "Using the wonders of
(11)
natural science to inspire city kids," indicates the intended audience.

Attention-getting techniques include the use of color, with burnt umber
(12)
framing the page, color tabs at the top of the page, and a colored sidebar
along the left margin. The Web site includes several links to related sites.
(13)

The most entertaining site plays a video about the fossil. Against a swampy
(14)   (15)
background the fossil skull appears, followed by the complete skeleton

visible within a huge crocodile; the grunting call of a crocodile is heard in

the background. Lettering about the age of the fossil (110 million years)
(16)
and the beast's length (40 feet) appears in the center of the screen and then

slowly stretches the full width of the screen to emphasize the magnitude of

these numbers. The magazine article includes additional information about
(17)
the discovery of the remains and the basis for the scientists' conclusions

about the beast's size and diet. The viewer of the Web site video can almost
(18)
smell the water-soaked vegetation and stagnant water of the swamp.

The *Science News* article includes paragraphs of factual information,
(19)
while the Project Exploration Web site includes little text but lots of eye-

catching color and graphics, as well as video and sound. While limited in
(20)
how they present information, print media often include large blocks of fac-

tual information. The Web site, in common with many others, refers view-
(21)
ers to related sites that provide additional information. Though limited in
(22)
how it presents information, this scientific magazine article is a more

authoritative source for a research paper than the Web site is.

1 Which sentence would BEST open the essay?

A   When they think of fossils, most people do not think of crocodiles.

B   Many people are interested in fossils, especially those left behind by huge creatures.

C   Do you want to meet a creature who considered dinosaurs mere morsels upon which to snack?

D   Modern crocodiles are relatively small when compared to one of their ancient, distant cousins.

2 What is the BEST way to write a Web site presentation of the story in sentence 3?

A   a scientific Web site presentation of the story

B   Project Exploration's Web site presentation of the story

C   a Web site story directed at middle school and high school students

D   Leave as is.

GO ON

3 Which sentence should follow sentence 3 to provide a thesis statement?

A   The print story includes quotations from scientists specializing in this field.

B   The Web site is more interesting, because it includes a video clip.

C   The Web site uses color and icons to engage the viewer's attention.

D   The print story provides more scientific information, but the Web site is more entertaining.

4 What is the BEST way to write The magazine article's catchy title appeals to the reader?

A   The magazine article's catchy title appeals to the reader, "Fossils Indicate . . . Wow, What a Crocodile!,"

B   The title of the magazine article appeals to the reader,

C   The magazine article's catchy title, "Fossils Indicate . . . Wow, What a Crocodile!" appeals to the reader,

D   Leave as is.

5 What is the BEST way to write Vertebrate paleontologists are quoted to include specific references?

A   Vertebrate paleontologists Paul C. Sereno and Wann Langston are quoted

B   Scientists from two important universities are cited and quoted

C   Two different university scientists are quoted as authorities and used

D   Leave as is.

6 Which specific evidence would BEST follow sentence 8?

A   The fossil skull was found more than 160 kilometers from the nearest coastline.

B   The fossil skull is 1.5 meters long, while the modern-day crocodile skull is only 50 centimeters long.

C   Paleontologists first found the remains of this crocodile in the African country of Niger in the 1960s.

D   With its eyes and nostrils at the top of the skull, the crocodile probably lay underwater waiting to ambush prey.

7 What is the BEST way to elaborate upon sentence 12?

A   Describe the information found at links listed on this Web page.

B   List the e-mail address and the physical address of Project Exploration.

C   Describe the pictures and icons on this Web page.

D   Describe the colors of the tabs and the sidebar.

8 What is the BEST way to write sentences 13 and 14?

A   The Web site includes several links to related sites. A video about the fossil is played on one of the sites.

B   The Web site includes links to other sites. The sites are related. The most entertaining site plays a video about the fossil.

C   The Web site includes several links to related sites, with the most entertaining site playing a video about the fossil.

D   Leave as is.

9 **Which sentence should be moved to the second paragraph to improve the organization?**

   A   16

   B   17

   C   18

   D   20

10 **Which final impression should be added to the end of the essay?**

   A   Print media may provide more information, but Web site videos are more entertaining.

   B   Web sites can lead you to authoritative information.

   C   Some Web sites are seldom updated even though they are much easier to update than print media.

   D   Many people would rather watch a movie than read a book or magazine.

Writing Workshop: Analyzing a Short Story

DIRECTIONS The following is a rough draft of a short story analysis. It contains errors in development and organization. Some of the questions refer to underlined words or numbered sentences within the text. Read the essay and answer questions 1 through 10.

Setting in Poe's "The Fall of the House of Usher"

In his short story "The Fall of the House of Usher," Edgar Allan Poe
(1)
uses stylistic devices.

From the first sentence of the story, Poe uses diction and imagery to
(2)
create a sense of foreboding:

> During the whole of a dull, dark, and soundless day in the
>
> autumn of the year, when the clouds hung oppressively low in
>
> the heavens, I had been passing alone, on horseback, through a
>
> singularly dreary tract of country, and at length found myself, as
>
> the shades of the evening drew on, within view of the melancholy
>
> House of Usher.

Even a reader unfamiliar with Poe's stories is prepared for a sad tale. In the
(3)   (4)
second sentence, the narrator says that "with the first glimpse of the building, a sense of insufferable gloom pervaded my spirit." As the narrator
(5)
describes the house from a distance, he uses personification, a form of
figurative language, to intensify the sense of gloom and sadness hanging
over the scene. Not only is the house "melancholy," but its windows are
(6)
"eye-like." Personification of the house itself parallels the story's equation
(7)
of the house with the Usher family. The narrator describes his impression
(8)
upon first viewing the house as "an iciness, a sinking, a sickening of the
heart—an unredeemed dreariness of thought." Even viewing the house
(9)
from a different vantage point does not improve the narrator's impression
of the scene. The grounds in which the house is set also increase the sense
(10)
of foreboding. The first paragraph of the story ends with the narrator
(11)

GO ON

WRITING WORKSHOP TESTS

for **COLLECTION 6** `page 440` *continued* **ANALYZING A SHORT STORY**

viewing "with a shudder even more thrilling than before . . . the ghastly

tree-stems, and the vacant and eye-like windows."

As he approaches the house, the narrator sees that "[m]inute fungi over-
(12)
spread the whole exterior, hanging in a fine tangled web-work from the

eaves." A narrow crack extends from the roof to the foundation, hinting at
(13)
a literal interpretation of the story's title. Inside, somber tapestries hang on
(14)
the walls, and the floors are black. Poe's emphasis on the gloomy setting
(15)
prepares the reader for the sad tale of the Usher family. The somberness
(16)
of the setting is reflected in the history of the family and in recent events

affecting Roderick Usher and his twin sister. She is dying. As the narrator
(17)   (18)
leaves the house, following the deaths of Roderick and his sister, the crack

in the house widens and brings the entire house down.

The narrator's descriptions of the House of Usher from a distance
(19)
and as he approaches it and his descriptions of the interior of the house

establish a sense of foreboding. Poe's use of stylistic devices to reinforce
(20)
the somber setting creates an oppressively mournful mood appropriate to

the subject of the story.

1 **Which comment should open the essay to grab the reader's attention?**

A This story is one of Poe's best, so it is frequently included in anthologies.

B Several films have been based on Poe's stories, but the films are seldom faithful to the stories.

C For more than 150 years, one writer has thrilled readers with his dark, gloomy tales.

D Poe is not known for writing cheerful tales with happy endings.

2 **How should uses stylistic devices be written to include a conclusion about the literary elements?**

A uses stylistic devices throughout the story

B uses the stylistic devices most often used by poets

C uses stylistic devices that demonstrate what a skillful, imaginative writer he is

D uses stylistic devices to establish an ominous setting and to foreshadow unhappy events

3 What elaboration would BEST precede sentence 3?

A   The entire first paragraph of the story describes a gloomy scene.

B   Many of the words ("dark," "dreary," "shades") sound ominous.

C   The narrator is riding alone and is therefore easily depressed.

D   Autumn can be a sad time of year, with the leaves falling.

4 What supporting details would BEST follow sentence 10?

A   a summary of plot events

B   a description of Roderick Usher, the narrator's friend

C   quotations describing the grounds in which the house is set

D   quotations from the conversation between the narrator and Roderick

5 Which sentence should begin the third paragraph to identify a key point?

A   A closer inspection of the house reinforces the gloomy impression.

B   The house is spooky no matter how it is viewed or from what distance.

C   The narrator is not dreaming or imagining a gloomy atmosphere.

D   The narrator crosses a causeway and enters the house under an arch.

6 What is the BEST change to sentence 17?

A   Change **She** to **His twin sister**.

B   Change **She** to **and his twin sister** and add to sentence 16.

C   Change **She** to **who** and add the clause to the end of sentence 16.

D   Leave as is.

7 What elaboration would BEST follow sentence 18?

A   The narrator is so eager to leave the house that he flees during a storm.

B   Both the deaths and the collapse of the house are foreshadowed by descriptions of the setting.

C   From nearby, the narrator watches the walls of the house fall into a small lake in front of the house.

D   The title of the story hints at this conclusion, a strategy common in Poe's stories.

8 Which clause should be added to the end of sentence 19 to complete the summary of key points?

A   that indicates Poe's state of mind

B   that is common in Poe's stories

C   that prepares the reader for the ending

D   that does not provide any laughs

9 What is the BEST way to revise sentence 20 as a restatement of the thesis?

A   Identify the stylistic devices discussed.

B   Include a brief summary of the plot.

C   Mention the relationship between Roderick and his sister.

D   Briefly describe the house.

10 What is the BEST general comment to add to the end of the essay?

A   Most of Poe's poems are also gloomy, with beautiful rhythms.

B   Though a U.S. writer and poet, Poe is often considered European in style.

C   Poe is often given credit for creating the modern detective story.

D   His word pictures are more vivid than many paintings.

for **COLLECTION 7**   *page 540*

Writing Workshop: Describing a Person

DIRECTIONS The following is a rough draft of a descriptive essay about a local baker. It contains errors in development and organization. Some of the questions refer to underlined words or numbered sentences within the text. Read the essay and answer questions 1 through 10.

The Bakery Lady

Mrs. Grundel immigrated to the United States with her parents more
(1)
than forty-six years ago, when she was just a child. Until we were old
(2)
enough to know better, my friends and I called her the Bakery Lady

because she owns Grundel's Bakery, a small shop on the corner of First

and Main Street. However, Mrs. Grundel is no ordinary baker.
(3)
Any time you speak with Mrs. Grundel, you can rely on her pinning
(4)
you with a strong look that lets you know you have her undivided atten-

tion. Wide brown eyes lift at the corners and seem to know things about
(5)
you without your telling her. "You've had a goot day," Mrs. Grundel will
(6)
say with authority as she pats you gently on the shoulder; or, "Vhat is

wrong?" she will ask, her twinkling eyes turning to a look of concern as

she sits down next to you. I suspect that Mrs. Grundel knows everyone's
(7)
secrets, for her honest concern compels people to talk.

As you walk into Grundel's, you can be assured that Mrs. Grundel will
(8)
stop what she is doing and greet you with a "Hallo" and a ready smile.

Then, when she's finished with what she is doing, she glides over to your
(9)
table. She is short and thin, quick and energetic. Though her dress is
(10)   (11)
usually brown, blue, or black, Mrs. Grundel always wears a brightly

colored apron in a flowery print tied around her tiny waist. I asked her
(12)
once why she wears the flowery aprons. She said they make her want
(13)
to smile.

For example, the day I had an argument with my best friend, Kent, I
(14)
went to the bakery and poured out all my troubles to Mrs. Grundel. She
(15)

GO ON ➡

was wearing pearl-pink nail polish that day. She arched one thin eyebrow,
(16)

gave me a stern but compassionate look, and said, "You must apologize

to your friend." Then she smiled knowingly. "Tomorrow, I make you
(17)   (18)

cinnamon buns. Bring Kent. You vill eat them together."
(19)   (20)

    I didn't like what Mrs. Grundel told me to do, but some inner voice told
(21)

me she was right. The next day, when Kent and I arrived at the bakery,
(22)

Mrs. Grundel smiled at us and then gave us each a warm hug. True to her
(23)

word, she placed a plate of large, still-warm cinnamon buns in front of

Kent and me.

    Mrs. Grundel moves about as though all of her energy is controlled by
(24)

some computer program designed for the utmost efficiency. Her small feet
(25)

do not shuffle but step firmly and purposely. She rarely wastes energy or
(26)

time with her hands. If they are not patting someone on the shoulder or
(27)

setting food and drinks on a table, then they are folded neatly in front of

her waist.

    Efficient and compassionate—that's how I would describe Mrs.
(28)

Grundel. Since I can remember, she has kept her bakery running smoothly
(29)

while being what many of us forget to be or rarely think about being—a

good neighbor. I've never met anyone who seemed to truly care about her
(30)

friends and neighbors as Mrs. Grundel does.

GO ON

WRITING WORKSHOP TESTS

1 **Which question, if added to the beginning of the essay, would BEST attract readers' attention?**

A Have you been to a bakery and tasted mouthwatering, home-baked bread?

B Have you ever met someone you truly admired, talked to all the time, and liked to visit on the weekends?

C Wouldn't you like to meet someone who bakes bread that melts in your mouth and who looks like the perfect grandmother?

D Do you know the baker in your neighborhood?

2 **Which sentence should be added to the end of the first paragraph to establish the controlling impression?**

A Although surrounded by work, Mrs. Grundel is never too busy to show she cares about the people around her.

B Mrs. Grundel is a respected member of our community and has lived here for the past forty-six years.

C She is a woman everyone in town adores, and many townspeople have known her since they were small children.

D There is much to like about Mrs. Grundel, and many people can tell stories about how she has helped them.

3 **How should strong look in sentence 4 BEST be written?**

A steady look

B piercing gaze

C long stare

D Leave as is.

4 **What factual details would BEST be added after sentence 10?**

A She bakes the best bread and pastries in town.

B She lives near the bakery in a small apartment with blue curtains at the windows.

C Her hair is graying at the temples and is worn in a neat little bun.

D The bakery always smells of fresh-baked bread, one of my favorite scents.

5 **Which sentence would BEST replace sentence 13?**

A She said, "Flowers brighten up the day," and I agreed with her.

B She told me that she just likes flowers, even on her clothes, and that they always cheer her up.

C She told me that flowers always make her smile, even on rainy days.

D In her heavily accented English, she said, "Flowers make you smile even if you do not want to, yah?"

6 **Which paragraph should be moved to follow the third paragraph?**

A second

B fourth

C fifth

D sixth

GO ON ➡

7 **Which sentence should be added before sentence 14 to BEST make the writer's thoughts and feelings clear?**

A   She knows about the mail carrier's peach tree and about the store clerk's old dog.

B   She's a good listener and always gives sound advice, even if it is not what you want to hear.

C   Everyone talks to Mrs. Grundel, even Mr. Shipley, the toughest teacher in school.

D   I heard my mom tell our neighbor that Mrs. Grundel makes the best cinnamon buns in town.

8 **Which sentence should be deleted?**

A   11

B   12

C   15

D   16

9 **Which sentence should be added after sentence 25 to add concrete sensory details?**

A   She always dresses sensibly, in keeping with her personality.

B   Rather than sitting still, she is always busy.

C   She seems nervous today and out of sorts.

D   Her back is ramrod straight, reminding me of an army general.

10 **Which of the following sentences would be MOST appropriate to add to the end of the essay?**

A   My mom says Mrs. Grundel is a true gem.

B   I'm glad she finds the time to be so caring, because she makes everyone feel special.

C   Any time people move into the neighborhood, we tell them about Mrs. Grundel.

D   It must be hard to run a bakery and be so friendly.

for **COLLECTION 8**   *page 602*

Writing Workshop: Short Story

DIRECTIONS The following is a rough draft of a short story. It contains errors in development and organization. Some of the questions refer to an underlined word or numbered sentences within the story. Read the story and answer questions 1 through 10.

Things Aren't Always What They Seem

Two days ago, Ruth had received the call. She'd done it. The newspaper
(1)   (2)   (3)
editor's voice still <u>sounded</u> in her head: "Your article will appear in this

Sunday's paper. Good work." For a while, she had allowed herself to enjoy
            (4)   (5)
the thrill, but it was now Saturday—time to give her parents the news

before they read it firsthand in tomorrow's paper. They were going to flip.
                                                              (6)

An hour later, Ruth spoke to her parents. "Mom, Dad, I have something
(7)   (8)
to tell you." Her heart beat fast.
        (9)

"What is it, dear?" her mother asked. She didn't like the sound of her
(10)   (11)
daughter's voice. Ruth was nervous.
            (12)

"I, um . . ." Ruth cleared her throat and ignored the drummer who'd
(13)   (14)
moved from her chest into her stomach, his drumsticks beating so hard

they were making her nauseated. "That is . . . well . . ."
                                    (15)

"Just spit it out, Ruth." Her dad's voice had that hard edge it got when
(16)   (17)
he was annoyed.

"Stringing us along isn't helping." Her mother stood still now, giving
(18)   (19)
her "the look."

"I wrote an article about our family and submitted it to *The Dispatch*."
(20)
"And?" the hard edge prompted.
(21)
"And you'll be reading it in tomorrow's paper."
(22)
What followed was nothing short of an interrogation as Ruth's parents
(23)
drilled her with questions. What did the article say about them? Why had
                              (24)   (25)
she done such a thing? Why hadn't she told them? Ruth planned to visit
            (26)   (27)
her friend Jill that evening.

GO ON

When it was all over, Ruth felt more confused than ever. She'd expected
(28)
the drill. She hadn't expected that her parents might actually be pleased.
(29)
(30)
Even now, when the Sunday paper had come, Ruth still wasn't sure how
(31)
her parents felt. She was too scared, however, to leave her room to find out.
(32)
She was a soldier holed up in a bunker, waiting for the battle to begin.
(33)
The knock on her door made her jump. It opened. Ruth couldn't quite
(34) (35) (36)
identify the look her parents gave her as they walked in and sat down

beside her. Her dad lifted the newspaper toward her. "This is very good."
(37) (38)
"Yes, very good," added her mother.
(39)
"But . . .," Ruth began.
(40)
Both of her parents were smiling.
(41)
Ruth's throat felt like dry chalk, but she managed to ask, "Are you sure
(42)
you didn't mind what I said about Claire?"

"We're very proud of your sister—and you."
(43)
Her mother stood up. "Now, get up and get dressed. We're going to
(44) (45) (46)
celebrate."

Her parents left the room. Ruth stared, stupefied, at the closed door,
(47) (48)
and then a slow smile spread across her face. She leaped out of bed and
(49)
gave a loud "Woo-hoo!"

1 **Which word would BEST replace
sounded in sentence 3?**

   A   reviewed

   B   hurt

   C   grew

   D   echoed

2 **Which sentence should be added after
sentence 4 to establish the setting?**

   A   Now she really had to work hard.

   B   At fifteen, she was already beginning
an exciting career!

   C   Ruth decided to stay in bed a little
longer.

   D   Ruth wondered whether she had
done the right thing.

GO ON

WRITING WORKSHOP TESTS

3 **Which revision would BEST improve the beginning of the story?**

A   Add details to show why Ruth has not told her parents.

B   Add a summary of Ruth's article.

C   Add a plot summary.

D   Add information about Ruth's relationship with her sister.

4 **What is the BEST way to write sentence 7 to locate the scene?**

A   Soon, Ruth talked to her parents inside the house.

B   An hour later, Ruth went to the kitchen for breakfast.

C   An hour later, Ruth slid into her chair at the breakfast table.

D   Leave as is.

5 **What is the BEST way to write sentence 9?**

A   Her heart beat faster and faster until she felt she would faint.

B   Her heartbeat felt like the rapid tapping of drumsticks on her chest.

C   Usually she had a slow heartbeat, but now her heart beat faster and faster.

D   Leave as is.

6 **Which sentence should be deleted to maintain a consistent point of view?**

A   8

B   10

C   11

D   14

7 **What should be added to the beginning of sentence 20 to provide sensory details to develop the character?**

A   A dog barked somewhere outside, and Ruth said,

B   Ruth spoke just as the phone rang:

C   The tension in the room was thick as Ruth said,

D   Ruth straightened her shoulders and blurted out,

8 **Which sentence should be deleted to remove irrelevant events?**

A   23

B   24

C   25

D   27

9 **What is the BEST revision to make following sentence 42?**

A   Add a summary of Ruth's sister's accomplishments.

B   Add dialogue that explains why Claire is significant.

C   Add a description of the setting and the characters.

D   Add a summary of the plot and brief descriptions of the characters.

10 **What is the BEST sentence to add to the end of the story?**

A   Ruth had not realized that her parents would support her decision to become a journalist.

B   Her journalism teacher would be pleased with her success.

C   She would encourage other students to submit their articles to the newspaper.

D   Now she needed to start on her English research paper.

for **COLLECTION 9** | *page 690*

Writing Workshop: Research Paper

DIRECTIONS The following is a rough draft of a research paper about the historical background of folk songs about John Henry. The draft contains errors in development and organization. Some of the questions refer to numbered sentences within the text. Read the paper and answer questions 1 through 15.

1 **Which question would BEST help the writer narrow the focus of the paper?**

A When did the oral tradition begin?

B When was the steam drill invented?

C Was John Henry a real person?

D What was the source of the melodies of the folk songs?

2 **Which is a primary source that would be MOST helpful to the writer?**

A a dictionary of musical terms

B an encyclopedia entry about John Henry

C a CD of modern folk songs

D an online image of the first printed version of "John Henry"

The Steely Story of John Henry

Children know the words "Once upon a time." To children, they
(1)
promise an entertaining tale. To folklorists such as Jane Yolen, they offer a
(2)   (3)
glimpse into history and the oral tradition: "Folktales . . . carry with them

the thumbprints of history" (Yolen 5). The oral tradition is still alive today
(4)
in folk songs. Some stories change as they are sung over and over. One
(5)   (6)
story kept alive in folk songs is the tale of John Henry. This story of one
(7)
man's battle against a machine is based in fact, but several versions of the

song have developed over time. Singers have kept to the facts.
(8)
    The basic story of John Henry remains the same in all versions of the
(9)
song. John Henry is always a large, powerful man. He is admired for his
(10)   (11)
speed and his skill with a heavy hammer. John Henry agrees to compete
(12)
with a steam-powered drill. He participates in the fierce competition.
(13)
He beats the machine and then dies ("John Henry" 543). All versions of
(14)   (15)
the story stress John Henry's strength, courage, and determination. In all
(16)
versions, he is a hero.

The songs about John Henry are based in fact. Experts agree that a man
(17)   (18)
named John Henry was born into slavery in Virginia or North Carolina

around 1850. After the Civil War, the freed John Henry was hired by the
(19)
Chesapeake and Ohio Railroad as a steel driver, a worker who made holes

in rock by using a heavy hammer to drive steel drills or spikes into the

rock. According to the Web site John Henry—The Steel Driving Man, the
(20)
railroad was to run through Big Bend Mountain in West Virginia and was

such a huge project that it took a thousand men three years to complete.

While driving steel through Big Bend, John Henry was challenged by the
(21)
owner of a pneumatic drill, a new invention at that time. Some believe that
(22)
John Henry died of exhaustion or from a stroke after the contest (Hempel,

Procopio, Shaver, and Novak). By the time the songs were first recorded in
(23)
1909, several versions had developed. Each has a different focus that
(24)
reveals something about the people who enjoyed it. In one, Henry's hero-
(25)
ism comes from being an African American who dared to test his strength

against a machine run by a white man (Hempel, Procopio, Shaver, and

Novak). Zora Neale Hurston, a collector of African American folk tales,
(26)
disagrees, however, about the song's ties to the African American tradition.

In fact, the version Hurston includes in her book Mules and Men does not
(27)
even mention that John Henry was African American or that the steam drill

operator was white (257–259).

    The story of John Henry appears to have its deepest ties to the tradition
(28)
of workers. The versions of the song within this tradition emphasize John
(29)
Henry's feat as a man who beats a machine that threatened the jobs of

railroad workers. The song was sung by workers of all types who prized
(30)
the story of the determined man and the clear rhythms of the song.

"[T]he song also reflects many faces, many lives. Some consider it a
(31)   (32)
protest anthem, an attempt by the laborers to denounce—without facing

GO ON

punishment or dismissal by their superiors—the wretched conditions

under which John Henry worked" (Hempel, Procopio, Shaver, and Novak).

Clearly all the versions of the story of John Henry have their place in
(33)
U.S. history and culture. Today, the story is often taught in literature classes
(34)
and appears quaint to young readers who will never have to pick up a

steel-driving hammer. However, for more than one hundred years, the
(35)
story of John Henry has inspired many people. Perhaps today's students
(36)
should take another look at John Henry and be inspired, too.

Works Cited

Hempel, Carlene, Deb Procopio, Dan Shaver, and Beth Novak. John

Henry—The Steel Driving Man. University of North Carolina—

Chapel Hill. 10 Nov. 2001 <http://www.ibiblio.org/john_henry>.

Hurston, Zora Neale. Mules and Men. Bloomington, IN: Indiana

University Press, 1935, 1978.

"John Henry." Benet's Reader's Encyclopedia of American Literature.

1st ed., 1991. Infotrac. 10 Nov. 2001 <http://

web1.infotrac.galegroup.com/itw/infomark /584/466/

17984626w1/puri=>.

Yolen, Jane, ed. Favorite Folktales from Around the World. New York:

Pantheon Books, 1986.

GO ON

3 **How should sentence 1 be written to create interest?**

A   Anyone who has been a child knows the thrill of the words "Once upon a time."

B   "Once upon a time" are words any child knows.

C   Children are familiar with folk tales and the opening, "Once upon a time."

D   Folk tales and folk songs are part of the oral tradition.

4 **Which sentence should be added after sentence 7 to indicate a main point to be discussed?**

A   Songs can definitely change over time.

B   There are many songs that tell the stories of our country's history.

C   Most versions place the song in the tradition of workers' songs.

D   Singing songs is one way to keep the American folk-song tradition alive.

5 **What is the BEST revision of sentence 8 as a thesis statement?**

A   Singers have kept to the facts, and so the song has never really changed.

B   Singers have kept to the facts, which their audiences must have always appreciated.

C   Singers have kept to the facts but have often changed the details to inspire their listeners.

D   Leave as is.

6 **What detail should be added after sentence 9?**

A   In some versions of the story, John Henry named his famous hammer after his wife, Lucy.

B   In one version, John Henry has a wife and baby boy.

C   One version starts with John Henry as a baby.

D   John Henry is always a worker building railroads after the Civil War.

7 **What is the BEST way to combine sentences 13–14?**

A   He participates in the fierce competition, while he beats the machine and then he dies.

B   When he participates in the fierce competition, he beats the machine and then dies.

C   He beats the machine after the fierce competition he competes in and then dies.

D   Leave as is.

8 **Which sentence in paragraph 3 should begin a new paragraph?**

A   20

B   22

C   23

D   25

GO ON

WRITING WORKSHOP TESTS

9 **Which sentence should be added after sentence 26 to BEST summarize Hurston's opinion?**

A Hurston gathered African American folk tales during her travels around the South in the 1930s.

B Hurston knew better than anyone else how to classify the folk song about John Henry.

C Hurston made lasting friendships with people she met by singing her favorite version of the ballad "John Henry."

D She claims that the song was primarily a work song with little connection to African American tradition.

10 **What is the correct reference to the book cited in sentence 27?**

A in her book called Mules and Men

B in her book Mules and Men

C in the book she wrote about this

D in her book "Mules and Men"

11 **What phrase or clause, if any, should be added to the beginning of sentence 31 to show the source of the quotation?**

A I think that the author was right for saying,

B Almost all U.S. folk song experts believe that

C According to John Henry—The Steel Driving Man,

D Leave as is.

12 **Which sentence should follow sentence 32 to summarize workers' responses to the song?**

A Even now, when steel driving is a task of the past, people enjoy songs about John Henry.

B The legend of John Henry is a part of the history of U.S. railroad workers.

C This quotation is from the Web site John Henry—The Steel Driving Man.

D Workers felt the song spoke for them.

13 **Which sentence should be added after sentence 33 to summarize the main points?**

A The oral tradition lives on in folk songs in all cultures and all countries.

B Singers have used different versions of this factually based story to inspire different audiences.

C Folk songs are enjoyed for their melodies as well as for the stories they relate.

D Some versions of "John Henry" tell of the struggles of African American working people.

GO ON

14 **What is the BEST revision of sentence 35 as a restatement of the thesis?**

A   However, the story of John Henry has inspired African American workers for more than one hundred years.

B   However, for more than one hundred years, different versions of the story of John Henry have inspired workers from many backgrounds.

C   However, the story of John Henry has led workers to seek better working conditions.

D   Understanding the importance of the story of John Henry for workers will help students understand U.S. history.

15 **Which sentence, if added at the end of the paper, would provide the BEST final insight?**

A   Maybe they will think twice next time they hear the story of John Henry!

B   Maybe students should consider the meaning behind their favorite songs.

C   Maybe students should join a folk song club and start collecting songs that are meaningful to them.

D   You need not be a steel driver to learn from John Henry's example.

Writing Workshop: Comparing a Play and a Film

DIRECTIONS The following is a rough draft of an essay comparing a scene in a film version of *Much Ado About Nothing* to the same scene in Shakespeare's play of the same name. The essay contains errors in development and organization. Some of the questions refer to underlined phrases or numbered sentences within the text. Read the essay and answer questions 1 through 10.

Much Ado About—What?

In his film adaptation of *Much Ado About Nothing*, director Kenneth
(1)
Branagh is very faithful to the script of the original play. However, his
(2)
narrative and film techniques, particularly in the crucial scene in which
Benedick overhears other characters discussing Beatrice's feelings for him
(act 2, scene 3), alter the emphasis of the play.

To emphasize the comic and romantic elements of the play, Branagh cuts
(3)
act 2, scene 2, a dark scene in which two characters conspire to spoil the
marriage plans of Claudio and Hero. As a result, the scene in which Don
(4)
Pedro and other characters stage a conversation about Beatrice's love so
that Benedick will hear it follows the scene in which Don Pedro develops
his plan to match Benedick and Beatrice romantically. This director's deci-
(5)
sion emphasizes the relationship between Benedick and Beatrice, whose
verbal fencing has already revealed their equality in intelligence and wit
and their emotional connection. Significantly, lines referring to the engage-
(6)
ment and impending marriage of Claudio and Hero are deleted, further
narrowing the focus to Benedick and Beatrice.

Stage directions for the play do not tell where this scene is located,
(7)
but Benedick says that he is in an orchard (2.3.4). In the film, the scene is
(8)
changed to a formal garden that includes a fountain and gravel walks lined
by trees. When the scene opens, Benedick is sitting in a folding canvas
(9)
chair next to the fountain. While delivering a soliloquy on the reasons he
(10)

GO ON

does not wish to marry, he sees Don Pedro and other characters approaching, takes his chair, and hides.

Benedick is meant to overhear the conversation, and as he eavesdrops, (11) his gestures and stage business with the chair reveal his changing thoughts about Beatrice and also emphasize the comic elements in the scene. Without such a prop, the filmmaker would need to switch the camera (12) back and forth between Benedick in his hiding place and the actors at the fountain; he would also need to zoom in on faces to reveal reactions. When (13) Don Pedro first mentions Beatrice's love for Benedick, Benedick falls out of the chair. For this bit of stage business, the camera need not zoom in on (14) Benedick's face to show his astonishment.

To encourage Benedick's growing attachment to Beatrice, Don Pedro (15) sends Beatrice to fetch Benedick to dinner. The stage direction simply says (16) "Enter Beatrice." In the film, Beatrice <u>enters in an angry manner</u> with a (17) fierce look on her face. The camera zooms in on her as she approaches and (18) then gives viewers a close-up shot of her face. It is clear to the viewer that (19) this errand is distasteful to her; however, since Benedick now believes that she loves him, he says to himself, "I do spy some marks of love in her" (2.3.242–243), a line that always draws a laugh from viewers.

Branagh employs narrative and film techniques <u>to emphasize some</u> (20) <u>elements of the play, at the expense of other elements</u>. In particular, the (21) elements of farce he adds to this scene place it—and the play—specifically in the genre of comedy. Branagh's embellishments are most clearly (22) represented by the chair, which allows him as the actor to demonstrate Benedick's changing feelings for Beatrice.

1 **Which sentence would BEST provide an interesting opener for the essay?**

A   Kenneth Branagh has made a few changes to *Much Ado About Nothing*.

B   Sometimes filmmakers change plays so that the original play is barely recognizable.

C   Who would think that a chair could do so much for a film?

D   How often do you watch films based on stage plays?

2 **Information that should be added to sentence 1 is that—**

A   film critics thought the film was faithful to the play

B   William Shakespeare wrote the play

C   Branagh has filmed many of Shakespeare's plays

D   this play is not as well known as some of Shakespeare's other plays

3 **How should alter the emphasis of the play BEST be written to provide a clear thesis statement?**

A   change the meaning of the play

B   shorten the play and make it more appropriate for a general film audience

C   give Branagh, who plays Benedick, a larger role in the film than in the play

D   emphasize the comedy and the romance while downplaying the darker elements of the play

4 **What supporting evidence would MOST appropriately follow sentence 5?**

A   an example of Benedick's and Beatrice's wit quoted from the play

B   a summary of the conspiratorial plan

C   a description of Claudio and Hero's wedding plans

D   an explanation of the relationship between Beatrice and Hero

5 **What is the BEST way to elaborate on sentence 6?**

A   Explain Don Pedro's role in the play and in the film.

B   Add a quotation announcing the approaching visitors.

C   Explain why the focus has been narrowed to Benedick and Beatrice.

D   Explain the marriage arrangements of Claudio and Hero.

6 **What should BEST be added to the end of sentence 10 to make the setting clear?**

A   so that he cannot be seen

B   behind some trees near the fountain

C   somewhere else in the garden

D   so that he can overhear the conversation

GO ON

WRITING WORKSHOP TESTS

7 **Which sentence should be added after sentence 12?**

A   On a stage, all actors would be visible to the audience during the entire scene.

B   The audience might be annoyed or confused by too many changes in camera angle and focus.

C   The fountain serves another important purpose when the love-stricken Benedick dances through it.

D   Use of the chair as a prop avoids the possibly confusing changes in camera direction.

8 **How should enters in an angry manner be revised to add sensory details?**

A   approaches Benedick angrily

B   enters, walking toward Benedick quickly and angrily

C   enters, striding angrily through the brilliantly green garden

D   walks toward Benedick looking displeased and angry

9 **How should to emphasize some elements of the play, at the expense of other elements be written to restate the thesis?**

A   to emphasize the comic elements of the play, at the expense of the darker, conspiratorial elements

B   not only to shorten the play but also to change its emphasis

C   to create a film that is generally faithful to Shakespeare's script but has a few significant changes

D   Leave as is.

10 **Which sentence provides the BEST closing thought for the essay?**

A   If you want to know what a play is really about, you should read the script.

B   Plays must often be cut because the script is too long to keep an audience's attention.

C   Branagh is also well known for his performances as Shakespearean characters.

D   Even a relatively small addition to a performance can significantly alter the tone of a play.

Writing: Business Letter

DIRECTIONS Vivian is interested in working as an intern this summer. Below is a draft of her business letter to a placement company's human resources department requesting information about the internships. Read the letter and answer questions 1 through 10.

Vivian Advocatus
830 Morningside Drive
Santa Cruz, CA 95065

Lotta Jobs Corporation
530 Career Street
Suite 980
Santa Cruz, CA

Hello, HR person,

I'm writing because I'm in high school and I want you to send me the scoop on jobs. Please send me everything you know about the internships that you give to kids who want to be ambitious and get good jobs. My school counselor said you've got the straight story on that kind of stuff, so that's why I'm writing to you this A.M. Thanks a million for helping me out in this way. I know one day I'll look back on this internship as a fantastic boost, so to speak, to my career, and I might be able to use some of your little interns myself someday.

Your friend and mine:

Vivian Advocatus

GO ON ➡

WRITING WORKSHOP TESTS

1 **To present the letter in block style, the heading, inside address, salutation, and body should be—**

A   centered

B   aligned left

C   aligned right

D   indented five spaces

2 **What should be added on the line under Vivian's address?**

A   Vivian's teacher's name

B   the title of the job Vivian wants

C   the date of the letter

D   Vivian's phone number

3 **What information should be added to the inside address?**

A   the name of the person who told Vivian about the internship

B   the name of Vivian's school

C   the company's phone number and e-mail address

D   the name, title, and position of the person to whom Vivian is writing

4 **Which salutation would BEST replace Hello, HR person,?**

A   Dear Human Resources Director:

B   Dear Sir,

C   Hello, HR Dept. and president,

D   To whom it may concern:

5 **The tone of the body of the letter would BEST be improved if Vivian—**

A   added more current student slang to show that her vocabulary is up-to-date

B   replaced short words with longer words

C   replaced contractions, slang, and informal expressions with formal vocabulary

D   changed "I" to "we" and "my" to "our" throughout the letter

6 **Lotta Jobs Corporation can send Vivian the MOST helpful information if Vivian adds to her letter—**

A   places she has visited

B   courses she thinks she might take next year

C   details about her parents' jobs and education

D   her relevant experience

7 **Vivian can BEST improve the organization of the body of her letter by—**

A   including an introduction with a specific request, a paragraph with background information, and a closing paragraph thanking the recipient

B   adding a separate paragraph about her hopes and dreams and the job she plans to seek when she graduates from college

C   adding a separate paragraph expressing appreciation for the school counselor who told her about the internship program

D   moving the thank-you sentence to the beginning of the letter

GO ON

8 How should the last sentence be written to maintain a business tone?

A This internship may help me get a great job.

B Someday, after I get a great job with the help of this internship, I may ask you for interns.

C I look forward to the day when I'll make tons of money because of the opportunity you're giving me, and then I'll need interns.

D This internship will help prepare me for a career that may enable me to provide a similar opportunity for other interns.

9 The closing <u>Your friend and mine:</u> is BEST written—

A Your friend,

B Sincerely,

C With love:

D Hoping to hear from you soon,

10 The alignment of the typed name should—

A be centered

B match the alignment of the body of the letter

C be at the right margin

D be where the writer chooses

Answer Sheet 1

Collection _____

Writing Workshop

1	Ⓐ	Ⓑ	Ⓒ	Ⓓ	**5**	Ⓐ	Ⓑ	Ⓒ	Ⓓ	**8**	Ⓐ	Ⓑ	Ⓒ Ⓓ
2	Ⓐ	Ⓑ	Ⓒ	Ⓓ	**6**	Ⓐ	Ⓑ	Ⓒ	Ⓓ	**9**	Ⓐ	Ⓑ	Ⓒ Ⓓ
3	Ⓐ	Ⓑ	Ⓒ	Ⓓ	**7**	Ⓐ	Ⓑ	Ⓒ	Ⓓ	**10**	Ⓐ	Ⓑ	Ⓒ Ⓓ
4	Ⓐ	Ⓑ	Ⓒ	Ⓓ									

Answer Sheet 2

Collection _____

Writing Workshop

1	Ⓐ Ⓑ Ⓒ Ⓓ		**6**	Ⓐ Ⓑ Ⓒ Ⓓ		**11**	Ⓐ Ⓑ Ⓒ Ⓓ
2	Ⓐ Ⓑ Ⓒ Ⓓ		**7**	Ⓐ Ⓑ Ⓒ Ⓓ		**12**	Ⓐ Ⓑ Ⓒ Ⓓ
3	Ⓐ Ⓑ Ⓒ Ⓓ		**8**	Ⓐ Ⓑ Ⓒ Ⓓ		**13**	Ⓐ Ⓑ Ⓒ Ⓓ
4	Ⓐ Ⓑ Ⓒ Ⓓ		**9**	Ⓐ Ⓑ Ⓒ Ⓓ		**14**	Ⓐ Ⓑ Ⓒ Ⓓ
5	Ⓐ Ⓑ Ⓒ Ⓓ		**10**	Ⓐ Ⓑ Ⓒ Ⓓ		**15**	Ⓐ Ⓑ Ⓒ Ⓓ

Answer Key

Collection 1

Autobiographical Narrative

p. 3

1. B (attention-grabbing opener)
2. C (specific modifiers)
3. A (background information)
4. D (meaning of experience)
5. C (factual detail)
6. A (relevant information)
7. B (logical order)
8. C (writer's thoughts)
9. D (figurative language)
10. B (significance of experience)

Collection 2

Biographical Narrative

p. 6

1. D (background information)
2. D (significance of subject)
3. A (setting)
4. B (organization)
5. C (sensory details)
6. B (controlling impression)
7. D (thoughts and feelings)
8. C (precise adverbs)
9. B (controlling impression)
10. A (significance of subject)

Collection 3

Analyzing Problems and Solutions

p. 9

1. C (attention-grabbing opener)
2. D (background information)
3. A (thesis statement)
4. B (supporting evidence)
5. C (example)
6. C (clichés replaced)
7. A (example)
8. C (restatement of thesis)
9. D (call to action)
10. C (emotional appeal)

Collection 4

Persuasive Essay

p. 12

1. C (attention-grabbing opener)
2. B (background information)
3. A (clear opinion statement)
4. A (relevant evidence)
5. C (effective organization)
6. C (effective organization)
7. B (active voice)
8. D (relevant evidence)
9. B (restatement of opinion)
10. D (call to action)

Answer Key (continued)

Collection 5

Comparing Media Genres

p. 15

1. C (interesting opener)
2. B (introduction of media)
3. D (thesis statement)
4. C (specific references)
5. A (specific references)
6. B (specific evidence)
7. D (elaboration)
8. C (varied sentence lengths)
9. B (logical organization)
10. A (final impression)

Collection 6

Analyzing a Short Story

p. 19

1. C (interesting comment)
2. D (thesis statement)
3. B (elaboration)
4. C (supporting details)
5. A (key point)
6. C (adjective clauses)
7. B (elaboration)
8. C (summary of key points)
9. A (restatement of thesis)
10. D (general comment)

Collection 7

Describing a Person

p. 22

1. C (attract readers' attention)
2. A (controlling impression)
3. B (precise nouns and adjectives)
4. C (sensory and factual details)
5. D (factual details)
6. A (spatial order)
7. B (thoughts and feelings)
8. C (details that support controlling impression)
9. D (figurative details)
10. B (final comment about subject)

Collection 8

Short Story

p. 26

1. D (action verbs)
2. C (setting)
3. A (introduction of conflict)
4. C (specific place)
5. B (figurative language)
6. C (consistent point of view)
7. D (sensory details)
8. D (relevant plot events)
9. B (logical resolution of conflict)
10. A (theme)

Answer Key *(continued)*

Collection 9

Research Paper

p. 29

1. C (prewriting: research questions)
2. D (prewriting: primary sources)
3. A (attention-getting opener)
4. C (main points)
5. C (thesis statement)
6. D (supporting details)
7. B (complex sentences)
8. C (main points in separate paragraphs)
9. D (summary)
10. B (citations)
11. C (integrating quotations)
12. D (summary of research)
13. B (summary of main points)
14. B (restatement of thesis)
15. D (final insight)

Collection 10

Comparing a Play and a Film

p. 35

1. C (engaging opening)
2. B (introduction of playwright)
3. D (thesis statement)
4. A (supporting evidence)
5. C (elaboration)
6. B (supporting evidence)
7. D (elaboration)
8. C (sensory details)
9. A (restatement of thesis)
10. D (closing thought)

Collection 11

Business Letter

p. 39

1. B (proper format)
2. C (proper format)
3. D (clear information)
4. A (courtesy)
5. C (formal tone)
6. D (clarity)
7. A (organization)
8. D (formal tone)
9. B (style)
10. B (proper format)

Workshop Scales and Rubrics

for **COLLECTION 1** *page 56*

ANALYTICAL SCALE

Writing: Autobiographical Narrative

Use the chart below (and the rubric on pages 50–51) to evaluate an autobiographical narrative. Circle the numbers that best indicate how well the criteria are met. With these ten criteria, the lowest possible score is 0, the highest 40.

4 = Clearly meets this criterion

3 = Makes a serious effort to meet this criterion and is fairly successful

2 = Makes some effort to meet this criterion but with little success

1 = Does not achieve this criterion

0 = Unscorable

▶ CRITERIA FOR EVALUATION	▶ RATING			
▶ Genre, Organization, and Focus				
Introduction grabs the readers' attention.	4	3	2	1
Introduction provides necessary background information.	4	3	2	1
Introduction hints at the significance of the experience.	4	3	2	1
Events are organized logically and are relevant to the experience.	4	3	2	1
Sensory and factual details about people, places, thoughts, and feelings support the controlling impression.	4	3	2	1
Figurative language and precise action verbs are used.	4	3	2	1
Specific modifiers create clear, vivid images.	4	3	2	1
Conclusion ends with a direct statement of the significance of the experience.	4	3	2	1
▶ Language Conventions				
Standard English spelling, punctuation, capitalization, and manuscript form are used appropriately for this grade level.	4	3	2	1
Standard English sentence and paragraph structure, grammar, usage, and diction are used appropriately for this grade level.	4	3	2	1
Total Points:				

WORKSHOP SCALES AND RUBRICS

for **COLLECTION 1**   *page 56*   **ANALYTICAL SCORING RUBRIC**

Writing: Autobiographical Narrative

WORKSHOP SCALES AND RUBRICS

CRITERIA FOR EVALUATION	SCORE POINT 4	SCORE POINT 3	SCORE POINT 2	SCORE POINT 1
Genre, Organization, and Focus				
Introduction grabs the readers' attention.	Introduction grabs the readers' attention with an interesting opener.	Introduction is interesting and takes readers into account.	Introduction is relevant but does not take readers' interests into account.	Introduction is dull.
Introduction provides necessary background information.	Necessary background information helps readers understand significance of experience.	Background information is necessary but insufficient.	Sparse background information is too limited to help readers understand the situation.	No useful background information is provided.
Introduction hints at the significance of the experience.	Introduction clearly hints at the significance of the experience.	Hint of the significance of the experience is difficult to determine.	Introduction vaguely mentions the significance of the experience.	No hint of the significance of the experience is given in the introduction.
Events are organized logically and are relevant to the experience.	Events relevant to the experience are organized in a logical sequence, usually chronological order or flashback.	Organization of events is mostly logical, and few irrelevant events are included.	Organization of events is unclear, and many irrelevant events are included.	Organization of events is confusing, with numerous irrelevant events.
Sensory and factual details about people, places, thoughts, and feelings support the controlling impression.	Concrete sensory and factual details about people, places, thoughts, and feelings strongly support the controlling impression.	Descriptions of thoughts and feelings and sensory and factual details adequately support controlling impression.	Sensory and factual details are inadequate to support controlling impression.	Sensory and factual details are extremely sparse, and narrative contains no descriptions of thoughts and feelings.
Figurative language and precise action verbs are used.	Figurative language (similes, metaphors, personification) and precise action verbs are used consistently to describe experience clearly.	Narrative includes some figurative language and precise action verbs to describe experience.	Narrative includes very little figurative language or precise action verbs.	Figurative language is missing, and vague language is used to describe events and actions.
Specific modifiers create clear, vivid images.	Specific modifiers that create clear, vivid images are used throughout the narrative.	Several specific, vivid modifiers are used.	Few specific modifiers are used.	Modifiers are vague and ineffective.

CRITERIA FOR EVALUATION	SCORE POINT 4	SCORE POINT 3	SCORE POINT 2	SCORE POINT 1
Conclusion ends with a direct statement of the significance of the experience.	Conclusion ends with a direct statement of the significance of the experience and clearly shows how the writer changed or what the writer learned.	Conclusion ends with a statement of the significance of the experience, but statement is general.	Conclusion ends with a vague statement of the significance of the experience.	Conclusion omits a statement of the significance of the experience.

Language Conventions

CRITERIA FOR EVALUATION	SCORE POINT 4	SCORE POINT 3	SCORE POINT 2	SCORE POINT 1
Standard English spelling, punctuation, capitalization, and manuscript form are used appropriately for this grade level.	Standard English spelling, punctuation, capitalization, and manuscript form are used appropriately for this grade level throughout the essay.	Standard English spelling, punctuation, capitalization, and manuscript form are used appropriately for this grade level, with few problems.	Inconsistent use of standard English spelling, punctuation, capitalization, and manuscript form disrupts readers' comprehension.	Minimal use of standard English spelling, punctuation, capitalization, and manuscript form confuses readers.
Standard English sentence and paragraph structure, grammar, usage, and diction are used appropriately for this grade level.	Standard English sentence and paragraph structure, grammar, usage, and diction are used appropriately for this grade level throughout the essay.	Standard English sentence and paragraph structure, grammar, usage, and diction are used appropriately for this grade level, with few problems.	Inconsistent use of standard English sentence and paragraph structure, grammar, usage, and diction disrupts readers' comprehension.	Minimal use of standard English sentence and paragraph structure, grammar, usage, and diction confuses readers.

WORKSHOP SCALES AND RUBRICS

ANALYTICAL SCALE

Speaking: Presenting a Narrative

Use the chart below to evaluate an oral narrative. Circle the numbers that best indicate how well the criteria are met. With ten criteria, the lowest possible score is 0, the highest 40.

4 = Clearly meets this criterion

3 = Makes a serious effort to meet this criterion and is fairly successful

2 = Makes some effort to meet this criterion but with little success

1 = Does not achieve this criterion

0 = Unscorable

▶ CRITERIA FOR EVALUATION	▶ RATING
▶ Content, Organization, and Delivery	
Introduction is intriguing and personal and encourages audience to identify with narrator.	4 3 2 1
Presentation is organized in the same introduction, body, and conclusion arrangement as written narrative.	4 3 2 1
Use of familiar vocabulary and concise sentences makes narrative easy to understand.	4 3 2 1
Strict chronological order is used to present the narrative.	4 3 2 1
Narrative includes concrete sensory details and specific locations.	4 3 2 1
Conclusion makes the significance of the experience clear and encourages audience to identify with experience.	4 3 2 1
An appropriate well-known quotation or an observation about life is included in the introduction and conclusion.	4 3 2 1
Narrative is delivered extemporaneously using prepared notes.	4 3 2 1
Verbal and nonverbal techniques enhance delivery.	4 3 2 1
▶ Language Conventions	
Standard English grammar, usage, and diction are used appropriately for this grade level.	4 3 2 1
Total Points:	

for **COLLECTION 2** *page 122*

ANALYTICAL SCALE

Writing: Biographical Narrative

Use the chart below (and the rubric on pages 54–55) to evaluate a biographical narrative. Circle the numbers that best indicate how well the criteria are met. With these twelve criteria, the lowest possible score is 0, the highest 48.

4 = Clearly meets this criterion

3 = Makes a serious effort to meet this criterion and is fairly successful

2 = Makes some effort to meet this criterion but with little success

1 = Does not achieve this criterion

0 = Unscorable

CRITERIA FOR EVALUATION	RATING
Genre, Organization, and Focus	
Narrative provides an interesting introduction to the subject.	4 3 2 1
Necessary background information is provided.	4 3 2 1
Introduction hints at significance of the subject.	4 3 2 1
Anecdotes contribute to controlling impression of the subject.	4 3 2 1
Concrete sensory details describe people and places.	4 3 2 1
Thoughts and feelings are described.	4 3 2 1
Precise adverbs enhance the narrative.	4 3 2 1
Narrative is logically organized and paced.	4 3 2 1
Conclusion reinforces controlling impression.	4 3 2 1
Conclusion sums up significance of the subject.	4 3 2 1
Language Conventions	
Standard English spelling, punctuation, capitalization, and manuscript form are used appropriately for this grade level.	4 3 2 1
Standard English sentence and paragraph structure, grammar, usage, and diction are used appropriately for this grade level.	4 3 2 1
Total Points:	

                                                      ANALYTICAL SCORING RUBRIC

Writing: Biographical Narrative

CRITERIA FOR EVALUATION	SCORE POINT 4	SCORE POINT 3	SCORE POINT 2	SCORE POINT 1
Genre, Organization, and Focus				
Narrative provides an interesting introduction to the subject.	Narrative opens with a striking and intriguing introduction to the subject that grabs readers' attention.	Narrative opens with an introduction to the subject that interests readers.	Opening is bland or unrelated to the subject.	Introduction to the subject is missing.
Necessary background information is provided.	All background information necessary for the specific audience is provided.	Some background information is provided but is insufficient for intended audience.	Background information provided is irrelevant or inappropriate.	Necessary background information is missing.
Introduction hints at significance of the subject.	Introduction includes an enticing hint of the subject's significance to writer.	Introduction includes a broad hint of the subject's significance to writer.	Introduction simply states the subject's significance.	Introduction contains no mention of the subject's significance to writer.
Anecdotes contribute to controlling impression of the subject.	Relevant, compelling anecdotes convincingly develop a single controlling impression of the subject.	Most anecdotes contribute to controlling impression of the subject.	At least one anecdote is related to controlling impression of the subject.	Anecdotes are missing or do not develop controlling impression of the subject.
Concrete sensory details describe people and places.	Vivid, concrete sensory details describe people and places.	Sensory details describe people and places.	Few sensory details are used to describe people and places.	Sensory details are missing.
Thoughts and feelings are described.	Thoughts and feelings of writer and others are clearly described by means of interior monologue and dialogue.	Thoughts and feelings of writer are described, but few thoughts and feelings of others are described.	Thoughts and feelings are vague.	Thoughts and feelings are omitted.
Precise adverbs enhance the narrative.	Precise, fresh adverbs enhance the entire narrative.	Several precise adverbs enhance the narrative, but some adverbs are worn out.	A few precise adverbs improve the narrative, but most adverbs are worn out.	Narrative contains only worn-out adverbs.

CRITERIA FOR EVALUATION	SCORE POINT 4	SCORE POINT 3	SCORE POINT 2	SCORE POINT 1
Narrative is logically organized and paced.	Anecdotes and events are in chronological order, descriptions are ordered clearly, and pacing is appropriate to time or mood.	For the most part, anecdotes and events are in chronological order, descriptions are ordered clearly, and pacing is appropriate to time or mood.	Anecdotes and events are presented in jumbled order, descriptions are hard to follow, and pacing is the same throughout.	Narrative has no logical organization of anecdotes or descriptions and no logical pacing.
Conclusion reinforces controlling impression.	Narrative ends with a memorable comment, image, or quotation that powerfully reinforces the controlling impression.	Narrative ends with a comment, image, or quotation that basically reinforces the controlling impression.	Narrative ends with a comment, image, or quotation that is unrelated to controlling impression.	Conclusion does not reinforce controlling impression.
Conclusion sums up significance of the subject.	Conclusion clearly sums up significance of the subject.	Conclusion states significance of the subject in a general way.	Conclusion merely hints at significance of the subject.	Conclusion ignores significance of the subject.
Language Conventions				
Standard English spelling, punctuation, capitalization, and manuscript form are used appropriately for this grade level.	Standard English spelling, punctuation, capitalization, and manuscript form are used appropriately for this grade level throughout the essay.	Standard English spelling, punctuation, capitalization, and manuscript form are used appropriately for this grade level, with few problems.	Inconsistent use of spelling, punctuation, capitalization, and manuscript form disrupts readers' comprehension.	Minimal use of spelling, punctuation, capitalization, and manuscript form confuses readers.
Standard English sentence and paragraph structure, grammar, usage, and diction are used appropriately for this grade level.	Standard English sentence and paragraph structure, grammar, usage, and diction are used appropriately for this grade level throughout the essay.	Standard English sentence and paragraph structure, grammar, usage, and diction are used appropriately for this grade level, with few problems.	Inconsistent use of sentence and paragraph structure, grammar, usage, and diction disrupts readers' comprehension.	Minimal use of sentence and paragraph structure, grammar, usage, and diction confuses readers.

for **COLLECTION 3** *page 212*

Writing: Analyzing Problems and Solutions

Use the chart below (and the rubric on pages 57–58) to evaluate a problem-solution analysis. Circle the numbers that best indicate how well the criteria are met. With these eleven criteria, the lowest possible score is 0, the highest 44.

4 = Clearly meets this criterion

3 = Makes a serious effort to meet this criterion and is fairly successful

2 = Makes some effort to meet this criterion but with little success

1 = Does not achieve this criterion

0 = Unscorable

CRITERIA FOR EVALUATION	RATING
Genre, Organization, and Focus	
Opening anecdote or example catches readers' attention.	4 3 2 1
Necessary background information is provided in introduction.	4 3 2 1
Thesis statement identifies problem and suggests solution.	4 3 2 1
Essay analyzes the problem, explains proposed solutions, and presents writer's suggested solution.	4 3 2 1
Reasons and evidence support the analysis.	4 3 2 1
Essay addresses readers' counterclaims.	4 3 2 1
Analysis uses straightforward or original language.	4 3 2 1
Conclusion reminds readers why writer's solution is best and restates thesis.	4 3 2 1
Conclusion contains call to action.	4 3 2 1
Language Conventions	
Standard English spelling, punctuation, capitalization, and manuscript form are used appropriately for this grade level.	4 3 2 1
Standard English sentence and paragraph structure, grammar, usage, and diction are used appropriately for this grade level.	4 3 2 1
Total Points:	

Writing: Analyzing Problems and Solutions

CRITERIA FOR EVALUATION	SCORE POINT 4	SCORE POINT 3	SCORE POINT 2	SCORE POINT 1
Genre, Organization, and Focus				
Opening anecdote or example catches readers' attention.	Opening anecdote or example is intriguing and catches readers' attention.	Opening anecdote or example interests readers.	Opening anecdote or example is bland or unrelated to problem or solution.	Opening ignores readers' interests.
Necessary background information is provided in introduction.	All necessary background information is provided in introduction.	Some relevant background information is provided but is insufficient.	Background information is unnecessary or irrelevant.	No necessary background information is provided.
Thesis statement identifies problem and suggests solution.	Thesis statement presents problem clearly and suggests writer's preferred solution.	Thesis statement vaguely identifies problem and suggests a solution.	Thesis statement is unclear and/or difficult to identify.	Thesis statement is missing.
Essay analyzes the problem, explains proposed solutions, and presents writer's suggested solution.	Essay provides a clear and complete analysis of the problem, explains proposed solutions, and presents writer's suggested solution.	Essay provides a fairly complete analysis of the problem, lists proposed solutions, and presents writer's suggested solution.	Essay incompletely analyzes the problem, and writer's solution is hard to identify.	Problem is not analyzed, and a solution is not presented.
Reasons and evidence support the analysis.	Strong reasons, precise, relevant evidence, and rhetorical devices convincingly support the analysis.	Reasons and evidence support the analysis, but rhetorical devices are used inappropriately.	Reasons and evidence are sparse.	No reasons or evidence supports the analysis.
Essay addresses readers' counterclaims.	Essay anticipates readers' potential objections, biases, misunderstandings, or counterclaims and convincingly addresses them.	Essay addresses most of readers' potential counterclaims.	Essay mentions counterclaims without addressing them.	Essay ignores readers' potential counterclaims.
Analysis uses straightforward or original language.	Analysis uses straightforward, original language, with no clichés.	Analysis generally uses straightforward language, with only a few clichés.	Analysis is marred by several clichés.	Analysis includes a distracting number of clichés.

WORKSHOP SCALES AND RUBRICS

CRITERIA FOR EVALUATION	SCORE POINT 4	SCORE POINT 3	SCORE POINT 2	SCORE POINT 1
Conclusion reminds readers why writer's solution is best and restates thesis.	Conclusion convincingly reminds readers why writer's solution is best and persuasively restates thesis in new and different way.	Conclusion reminds readers why writer's solution is best and restates thesis in the same words as in introduction.	Conclusion repeats thesis statement from introduction and does not remind readers why writer's solution is best.	Conclusion omits thesis statement and any mention of writer's solution.
Conclusion contains call to action.	Conclusion contains a specific call to action that invites readers to participate in writer's solution to problem.	Conclusion contains a call to action with no clear directive as to how readers could participate in solution.	Conclusion contains a weak call to action.	Conclusion omits call to action.
Language Conventions				
Standard English spelling, punctuation, capitalization, and manuscript form are used appropriately for this grade level.	Standard English spelling, punctuation, capitalization, and manuscript form are used appropriately for this grade level throughout the essay.	Standard English spelling, punctuation, capitalization, and manuscript form are used appropriately for this grade level, with few problems.	Inconsistent use of spelling, punctuation, capitalization, and manuscript form disrupts readers' comprehension.	Minimal use of spelling, punctuation, capitalization, and manuscript form confuses readers.
Standard English sentence and paragraph structure, grammar, usage, and diction are used appropriately for this grade level.	Standard English sentence and paragraph structure, grammar, usage, and diction are used appropriately for this grade level throughout the essay.	Standard English sentence and paragraph structure, grammar, usage, and diction are used appropriately for this grade level, with few problems.	Inconsistent use of sentence and paragraph structure, grammar, usage, and diction disrupts readers' comprehension.	Minimal use of sentence and paragraph structure, grammar, usage, and diction confuses readers.

for **COLLECTION 3** *page 220*   **ANALYTICAL SCALE**

Speaking: Giving a Persuasive Speech

Use the chart below to evaluate a persuasive speech. Circle the numbers that best indicate how well the criteria are met. With these eight criteria, the lowest possible score is 0, the highest 32.

4 = Clearly meets this criterion

3 = Makes a serious effort to meet this criterion and is fairly successful

2 = Makes some effort to meet this criterion but with little success

1 = Does not achieve this criterion

0 = Unscorable

CRITERIA FOR EVALUATION	RATING
Content, Organization, and Delivery	
Speech begins with thesis and presents speaker's opinion about problem and the best solution.	4 3 2 1
Reasons and evidence support proposed solution.	4 3 2 1
Reasons are presented in order of importance.	4 3 2 1
Listeners' concerns and counterarguments are addressed.	4 3 2 1
Speech ends with call to action.	4 3 2 1
Speaker uses only brief notes during delivery.	4 3 2 1
Speaker presents arguments with effective delivery techniques.	4 3 2 1
Language Conventions	
Standard English grammar, usage, and diction are used appropriately for this grade level.	4 3 2 1
Total Points:	

ANALYTICAL SCALE

Writing: Persuasive Essay

Use the chart below (and the rubric on pages 61–62) to evaluate a persuasive essay. Circle the numbers that best indicate how well the criteria are met. With these ten criteria, the lowest possible score is 0, the highest 40.

4 = Clearly meets this criterion

3 = Makes a serious effort to meet this criterion and is fairly successful

2 = Makes some effort to meet this criterion but with little success

1 = Does not achieve this criterion

0 = Unscorable

CRITERIA FOR EVALUATION	RATING
Genre, Organization, and Focus	
Introduction grabs readers' attention.	4 3 2 1
Introduction gives background information on the issue.	4 3 2 1
Opinion statement in introduction clearly states the position.	4 3 2 1
At least three reasons reflecting logical, emotional, or ethical appeals support the opinion statement.	4 3 2 1
At least two pieces of evidence support each reason.	4 3 2 1
Reasons are organized effectively.	4 3 2 1
Conclusion restates opinion.	4 3 2 1
Conclusion includes a call to action.	4 3 2 1
Language Conventions	
Standard English spelling, punctuation, capitalization, and manuscript form are used appropriately for this grade level.	4 3 2 1
Standard English sentence and paragraph structure (with emphasis on using active voice), grammar, usage, and diction are used appropriately for this grade level.	4 3 2 1
Total Points:	

WORKSHOP SCALES AND RUBRICS

Writing: Persuasive Essay

CRITERIA FOR EVALUATION	SCORE POINT 4	SCORE POINT 3	SCORE POINT 2	SCORE POINT 1
Genre, Organization, and Focus				
Introduction grabs readers' attention.	Introduction effectively grabs readers' attention by asking a question, relating an anecdote, or presenting a startling statistic.	Introduction generally appeals to readers.	Introduction acknowledges readers but does not engage their interest.	Introduction ignores readers.
Introduction gives background information on the issue.	Introduction gives relevant background information that helps readers understand the issue.	Introduction gives some background information relevant to the issue.	Introduction gives insufficient or irrelevant background information.	Introduction omits necessary background information.
Opinion statement in introduction clearly states the position.	Opinion statement in introduction clearly states the position on issue.	Opinion statement in introduction is somewhat general.	Opinion statement in introduction is weak or not specific to the issue.	Introduction omits opinion statement.
At least three reasons reflecting logical, emotional, and ethical appeals support the opinion statement.	At least three strong, relevant reasons reflecting logical, emotional, and ethical appeals support the opinion statement.	Relevant reasons reflecting logical, emotional, or ethical appeals support the opinion statement.	Only one reason supports the opinion, or reasons are not strong or relevant.	Reasons supporting the opinion are not included, or reasons are irrelevant.
At least two pieces of evidence support each reason.	At least two pieces of relevant and sufficient evidence (facts, examples, expert opinions, analogies, case studies, anecdotes) support each reason.	Relevant evidence (facts, examples, expert opinions, analogies, case studies, anecdotes) supports each reason, but some support is weak.	Little evidence supports each reason, evidence supports only a single reason, or support is weak.	No evidence supports any reason.
Reasons are organized effectively.	Reasons are plainly organized effectively, most likely in order of importance.	Reasons are generally organized effectively, with only minor lapses in order of importance.	Reasons only occasionally indicate an organizational pattern.	Reasons are in random order.

WORKSHOP SCALES AND RUBRICS

WORKSHOP SCALES AND RUBRICS

CRITERIA FOR EVALUATION	SCORE POINT 4	SCORE POINT 3	SCORE POINT 2	SCORE POINT 1
Conclusion restates opinion.	Conclusion clearly and freshly restates opinion.	Conclusion gives a general restatement of opinion.	Conclusion's restatement of opinion is unclear or simply repeats opinion statement from introduction.	Conclusion omits restatement of opinion.
Conclusion includes a call to action.	Conclusion includes a reasonable, direct, and specific call to action that tells readers what they can do to help change the situation.	Conclusion includes a reasonable and general call to action.	Conclusion includes an unrealistic or nonspecific call to action.	Conclusion omits a call to action or makes a call to action unrelated to the essay.
Language Conventions				
Standard English spelling, punctuation, capitalization, and manuscript form are used appropriately for this grade level.	Standard English spelling, punctuation, capitalization, and manuscript form are used appropriately for this grade level throughout the essay.	Standard English spelling, punctuation, capitalization, and manuscript form are used appropriately for this grade level, with few problems.	Inconsistent use of standard English spelling, punctuation, capitalization, and manuscript form disrupts readers' comprehension.	Minimal use of standard English spelling, punctuation, capitalization, and manuscript form confuses readers.
Standard English sentence and paragraph structure (with emphasis on using active voice), grammar, usage, and diction are used appropriately for this grade level.	Standard English sentence and paragraph structure (with emphasis on using active voice), grammar, usage, and diction are used appropriately for this grade level throughout the essay.	Standard English sentence and paragraph structure (with emphasis on using active voice), grammar, usage, and diction are used appropriately for this grade level, with few problems.	Inconsistent use of standard English sentence and paragraph structure, grammar, usage, and diction disrupts readers' comprehension.	Minimal use of standard English sentence and paragraph structure, grammar, usage, and diction confuses readers.

ANALYTICAL SCALE

Speaking: Participating in a Debate

Use the chart below to evaluate a debate. Circle the numbers that best indicate how well the criteria are met. With these five criteria for participation in a debate, the lowest possible score is 0, the highest 20.

4 = Clearly meets this criterion

3 = Makes a serious effort to meet this criterion and is fairly successful

2 = Makes some effort to meet this criterion but with little success

1 = Does not achieve this criterion

0 = Unscorable

CRITERIA FOR EVALUATION	RATING
Content, Organization, and Delivery	
Credible, valid, relevant evidence (facts, statistics, specific instances, and testimony) supports the proposition or refutation.	4 3 2 1
Rebuttal effectively responds to opposing argument.	4 3 2 1
Debate etiquette is followed.	4 3 2 1
Voice, facial expressions, and eye contact aid audience understanding and emphasize important points.	4 3 2 1
Language Conventions	
Standard English appropriate for this grade level is used.	4 3 2 1
Total Points:	

WORKSHOP SCALES AND RUBRICS

ANALYTICAL SCALE

Listening: Judging a Debate

Use the chart below to evaluate the judging of the debate. Circle the numbers that best indicate how well the criteria are met. With these five criteria for judging a debate, the lowest possible score is 0, the highest 20.

4 = Clearly meets this criterion

3 = Makes a serious effort to meet this criterion and is fairly successful

2 = Makes some effort to meet this criterion but with little success

1 = Does not achieve this criterion

0 = Unscorable

CRITERIA FOR EVALUATION	RATING
The Listener	
Evaluates content, including persuasiveness of analysis and solution	4 3 2 1
Evaluates credibility, validity, and relevance of evidence	4 3 2 1
Evaluates the effectiveness of rebuttals	4 3 2 1
Evaluates delivery, including confidence and preparation, eye contact, rate and volume, and observance of debate etiquette	4 3 2 1
Language Conventions	
Evaluates standard English grammar, usage, and diction	4 3 2 1
Total Points:	

for **COLLECTION 5** | page 382 |

Writing: Comparing Media Genres

Use the chart below (and the rubric on pages 66–67) to evaluate an essay comparing media genres. Circle the numbers that best indicate how well the criteria are met. With these twelve criteria, the lowest possible score is 0, the highest 48.

4 = Clearly meets this criterion

3 = Makes a serious effort to meet this criterion and is fairly successful

2 = Makes some effort to meet this criterion but with little success

1 = Does not achieve this criterion

0 = Unscorable

CRITERIA FOR EVALUATION	RATING
Genre, Organization, and Focus	
Essay starts with interesting opener.	4 3 2 1
Introduction includes necessary background information.	4 3 2 1
The two media to be compared and contrasted are introduced.	4 3 2 1
Thesis statement presents the conclusions about the media coverage.	4 3 2 1
Organization is easy to follow.	4 3 2 1
Each point of comparison is supported by specific details and references to the news stories.	4 3 2 1
Sentences are of varying lengths.	4 3 2 1
Conclusion summarizes main points by restating thesis.	4 3 2 1
Ideas are offered on how stories were shaped by the media.	4 3 2 1
Essay closes with final impression or insight.	4 3 2 1
Language Conventions	
Standard English spelling, punctuation, capitalization, and manuscript form are used appropriately for this grade level.	4 3 2 1
Standard English sentence and paragraph structure, grammar, usage, and diction are used appropriately for this grade level.	4 3 2 1
Total Points:	

for **COLLECTION 5** `page 382`   **ANALYTICAL SCORING RUBRIC**

Writing: Comparing Media Genres

WORKSHOP SCALES AND RUBRICS

CRITERIA FOR EVALUATION	SCORE POINT 4	SCORE POINT 3	SCORE POINT 2	SCORE POINT 1
Genre, Organization, and Focus				
Essay starts with interesting opener.	Essay starts with interesting opener that engages readers.	Essay starts with opener that interests some readers.	Essay opener is only partially successful in engaging readers.	Essay opener is dull.
Introduction includes necessary background information.	Introduction includes all necessary background information about the news event for the readers.	Introduction includes insufficient background information.	Introduction includes irrelevant background information.	Introduction includes no background information.
The two media to be compared and contrasted are introduced.	The two media to be compared and contrasted are clearly introduced.	The two media to be compared and contrasted are only generally introduced.	The two media to be compared and contrasted are difficult to identify.	The two media to be compared and contrasted are not mentioned in introduction.
Thesis statement presents the conclusions about the media coverage.	Clear, coherent thesis statement presents a supportable conclusion about the media coverage.	Thesis statement presents a clear conclusion about the media coverage.	Thesis statement is incomplete.	Introduction lacks thesis statement.
Organization is easy to follow.	Essay is easy to follow in a clear block, point-by-point, or modified block style.	Essay is organized in block, point-by-point, or modified block style, with few lapses.	Essay is somewhat organized, but lapses in order make it difficult to follow.	Essay is disorganized and confusing.
Each point of comparison is supported by specific details and references to the news stories.	Each point of comparison is supported by specific details, such as quotations and examples, and references to the news stories.	Most points of comparison are supported by specific details and references to the news stories.	A few points of comparison are supported by specific details and references to the news stories, but much support is missing.	Points of comparison are not supported by details or references to the news stories.
Sentences are of varying lengths.	Sentences of varying lengths help hold the readers' attention.	Essay occasionally has a few sentences of the same length in succession.	Many sentences are the same length.	Essay has almost no variation in sentence length.
Conclusion summarizes main points by restating thesis.	Conclusion clearly summarizes main points by freshly restating thesis.	Conclusion summarizes main points by restating thesis, but restatement is not clear.	Conclusion merely repeats thesis statement from introduction or contains only part of it.	Conclusion lacks restatement of thesis.

for **COLLECTION 5** page 382 *continued*   **ANALYTICAL SCORING RUBRIC**

CRITERIA FOR EVALUATION	SCORE POINT 4	SCORE POINT 3	SCORE POINT 2	SCORE POINT 1
Ideas are offered on how stories were shaped by the media.	Clear, precise ideas on how the two stories were shaped by the media are offered.	General ideas on how the two stories were shaped by the media are offered.	Ideas on how stories were shaped by the media are limited or incomplete.	Ideas on how stories were shaped by the media are omitted.
Essay closes with final impression or insight.	Essay closes with perceptive final impression or insight about the media being compared.	Essay closes with appropriate final impression or insight about the media being compared.	Essay closes with final impression or insight unrelated to the media being compared.	No final impression or insight is included.
Language Conventions				
Standard English spelling, punctuation, capitalization, and manuscript form are used appropriately for this grade level.	Standard English spelling, punctuation, capitalization, and manuscript form are used appropriately for this grade level throughout the essay.	Standard English spelling, punctuation, capitalization, and manuscript form are used appropriately for this grade level, with few problems.	Inconsistent use of spelling, punctuation, capitalization, and manuscript form disrupts readers' comprehension.	Minimal use of spelling, punctuation, capitalization, and manuscript form confuses readers.
Standard English sentence and paragraph structure, grammar, usage, and diction are used appropriately for this grade level.	Standard English sentence and paragraph structure, grammar, usage, and diction are used appropriately for this grade level throughout the essay.	Standard English sentence and paragraph structure, grammar, usage, and diction are used appropriately for this grade level, with few problems.	Inconsistent use of sentence and paragraph structure, grammar, usage, and diction disrupts readers' comprehension.	Minimal use of sentence and paragraph structure, grammar, usage, and diction confuses readers.

WORKSHOP SCALES AND RUBRICS

Writing: Analyzing a Short Story

Use the chart below (and the rubric on pages 69–70) to evaluate an analysis of a short story. Circle the numbers that best indicate how well the criteria are met. With these ten criteria, the lowest possible score is 0, the highest 40.

4 = Clearly meets this criterion

3 = Makes a serious effort to meet this criterion and is fairly successful

2 = Makes some effort to meet this criterion but with little success

1 = Does not achieve this criterion

0 = Unscorable

CRITERIA FOR EVALUATION	RATING
Genre, Organization, and Focus	
Essay opens with interesting comment on story.	4 3 2 1
Thesis statement in introduction identifies story's title and author, literary element(s) discussed, and conclusion about element(s).	4 3 2 1
Key points are identified and organized in body of analysis.	4 3 2 1
Details from story support each key point.	4 3 2 1
Elaboration connects key points and supporting details.	4 3 2 1
Adjective clauses help vary sentence length.	4 3 2 1
Conclusion summarizes key points and restates thesis.	4 3 2 1
A comment for readers to consider concludes essay.	4 3 2 1
Language Conventions	
Standard English spelling, punctuation, capitalization, and manuscript form are used appropriately for this grade level.	4 3 2 1
Standard English sentence and paragraph structure, grammar, usage, and diction are used appropriately for this grade level.	4 3 2 1
Total Points:	

ANALYTICAL SCORING RUBRIC

Writing: Analyzing a Short Story

CRITERIA FOR EVALUATION	SCORE POINT 4	SCORE POINT 3	SCORE POINT 2	SCORE POINT 1
Genre, Organization, and Focus				
Essay opens with interesting comment on story.	Essay opens with interesting comment on story that grabs reader's attention.	Essay opens with comment that interests some readers.	Essay opens with bland statement or a comment not connected to story.	Opening is dull and uninteresting.
Thesis statement in introduction identifies story's title and author, literary element(s) discussed, and conclusion about element(s).	Thesis statement in introduction specifically identifies story's title and author, literary element(s) discussed, and conclusion about specific literary element(s).	Thesis statement in introduction identifies story's title and author, but identification of and conclusion about literary element(s) lack clarity.	Thesis statement includes only some elements or is confusing and hard to follow.	Introduction omits thesis statement.
Key points are identified and organized in body of analysis.	Key points are clearly identified and organized in chronological order or by order of importance.	Key points are identified and generally organized in chronological order or by order of importance.	Several key points are identified, but organization of essay is hard to follow.	Key points are not identified and analysis is in random order.
Details from story support each key point.	Relevant details from story (direct quotations, summaries, paraphrases) support each key point.	Details from story (direct quotations, summaries, paraphrases) support most key points.	A few details from story support some key points, but some support is missing or not relevant to point discussed.	Details from story are not used for support.
Elaboration connects key points and supporting details.	Elaboration clearly explains how supporting details are related to each key point.	Elaboration usually connects key points and supporting details.	Elaboration only occasionally explains connections between details and key points.	Elaboration is missing.
Adjective clauses help vary sentence length.	Adjective clauses are skillfully used to vary sentence length.	Adjective clauses help vary sentence length, but a few short, choppy sentences need to be combined.	A few adjective clauses are used to vary sentence length, but numerous short, choppy sentences occur back-to-back.	Adjective clauses are not used to vary sentence length.

CRITERIA FOR EVALUATION	SCORE POINT 4	SCORE POINT 3	SCORE POINT 2	SCORE POINT 1
Conclusion summarizes key points and restates thesis.	Conclusion concisely summarizes key points and restates thesis with words different from those in introduction.	Conclusion generally summarizes key points and restates thesis.	Summary of key points and restatement of thesis statement are incomplete or one is missing.	Conclusion omits summary and restatement of thesis.
A comment for readers to consider concludes essay.	A comment related to thesis that leaves readers with something to consider concludes essay.	A comment related to thesis that interests readers concludes essay.	A comment unrelated to thesis concludes essay.	There is no comment on story or thesis at end of essay.

Language Conventions

	SCORE POINT 4	SCORE POINT 3	SCORE POINT 2	SCORE POINT 1
Standard English spelling, punctuation, capitalization, and manuscript form are used appropriately for this grade level.	Standard English spelling, punctuation, capitalization, and manuscript form are used appropriately for this grade level throughout the essay.	Standard English spelling, punctuation, capitalization, and manuscript form are used appropriately for this grade level, with few problems.	Inconsistent use of spelling, punctuation, capitalization, and manuscript form disrupts readers' comprehension.	Minimal use of spelling, punctuation, capitalization, and manuscript form confuses readers.
Standard English sentence and paragraph structure, grammar, usage, and diction are used appropriately for this grade level.	Standard English sentence and paragraph structure, grammar, usage, and diction are used appropriately for this grade level throughout the essay.	Standard English sentence and paragraph structure, grammar, usage, and diction are used appropriately for this grade level, with few problems.	Inconsistent use of sentence and paragraph structure, grammar, usage, and diction disrupts readers' comprehension.	Minimal use of sentence and paragraph structure, grammar, usage, and diction confuses readers.

WORKSHOP SCALES AND RUBRICS

Speaking: Presenting a Literary Response

Use the chart below to evaluate a presentation of a literary response. Circle the numbers that best indicate how well the criteria are met. With these nine criteria, the lowest possible score is 0, the highest 36.

4 = Clearly meets this criterion

3 = Makes a serious effort to meet this criterion and is fairly successful

2 = Makes some effort to meet this criterion but with little success

1 = Does not achieve this criterion

0 = Unscorable

CRITERIA FOR EVALUATION	RATING
Content, Organization, and Delivery	
Introduction uses quotation, personal observation, anecdote, or reference to familiar source to grab listeners' attention.	4 3 2 1
Introduction identifies story's title and author and the conclusion about the story element(s).	4 3 2 1
Elaboration of details about the important ideas in the story makes presentation easy to understand.	4 3 2 1
Transitional words and phrases guide listeners through presentation.	4 3 2 1
Conclusion summarizes the key points and restates the thesis with strong, simple language.	4 3 2 1
Presentation concludes with dramatic, personal statement that shows speaker's appreciation of the effects the author created in story.	4 3 2 1
Voice, gestures, eye contact, and facial expressions hold listeners' interest.	4 3 2 1
Oral response is presented extemporaneously, using notes.	4 3 2 1
Language Conventions	
Standard English grammar, usage, and diction are used appropriately for this grade level.	4 3 2 1
Total Points:	

Writing: Describing a Person

Use the chart below (and the rubric on pages 73–74) to evaluate a descriptive essay. Circle the numbers that best indicate how well the criteria are met. With these ten criteria, the lowest possible score is 0, the highest 40.

4 = Clearly meets this criterion

3 = Makes a serious effort to meet this criterion and is fairly successful

2 = Makes some effort to meet this criterion but with little success

1 = Does not achieve this criterion

0 = Unscorable

WORKSHOP SCALES AND RUBRICS

CRITERIA FOR EVALUATION	RATING
Genre, Organization, and Focus	
Introduction attracts readers' attention and presents person to be described.	4 3 2 1
Introduction includes a statement of the controlling impression.	4 3 2 1
Sensory, factual, and figurative details enhance the description.	4 3 2 1
Thoughts and feelings about the subject are included.	4 3 2 1
All details are related to the controlling impression.	4 3 2 1
Details are arranged by spatial order or by order of importance.	4 3 2 1
Precise nouns, verbs, and adjectives make the ideas clear.	4 3 2 1
Conclusion restates the controlling impression and summarizes the points of the description.	4 3 2 1
Language Conventions	
Standard English spelling, punctuation, capitalization, and manuscript form are used appropriately for this grade level.	4 3 2 1
Standard English sentence and paragraph structure, grammar, usage, and diction are used appropriately for this grade level.	4 3 2 1
Total Points:	

Writing: Describing a Person

CRITERIA FOR EVALUATION	SCORE POINT 4	SCORE POINT 3	SCORE POINT 2	SCORE POINT 1
▶ **Genre, Organization, and Focus**				
Introduction attracts readers' attention and presents person to be described.	Introduction effectively attracts readers' attention and clearly presents person to be described.	Introduction generally appeals to readers and presents person to be described.	Introduction acknowledges readers and mentions person to be described but is not engaging.	Introduction is dull, ignores readers' interests, or does not present person to be described.
Introduction contains a statement of the controlling impression.	Introduction contains a clear, specific statement of controlling impression of subject.	Introduction contains a general statement of controlling impression.	Introduction contains an unfocused statement about the subject.	Controlling impression is not stated.
Sensory, factual, and figurative details enhance the description.	A combination of concrete sensory, factual, and figurative details enhances the description and creates a complete portrait of the person.	Sensory, factual, and figurative details are scattered throughout the description.	Sparse sensory, factual, and figurative details leave readers without a clear idea of person.	Sensory, factual, and figurative details are omitted.
Thoughts and feelings about the subject are included.	Thoughts and feelings about the subject are clearly revealed.	Thoughts and feelings about the subject are generally mentioned.	Thoughts and feelings about the subject are vague or meager.	Thoughts and feelings about the subject are omitted.
All details are related to the controlling impression.	All details are clearly and directly related to the controlling impression.	Most details are generally related to the controlling impression.	Some details are related to the controlling impression, but many details are irrelevant.	Details are irrelevant or unclear, or very few details are present.
Details are arranged by spatial order or by order of importance.	All details are logically arranged, either by spatial order or by order of importance with effective transitions.	Details are arranged by spatial order or by order of importance, with only minor lapses.	Arrangement of details is not logical; few details are in spatial order or order of importance.	Details are in random order and are confusing to readers.
Precise nouns, verbs, and adjectives make the ideas clear.	Precise nouns, verbs, and adjectives make the image of the person crystal-clear throughout the description.	Precise nouns, verbs, and adjectives make the ideas and image clear in most of the description.	Precise nouns, verbs, and adjectives are seldom used.	Vague words make the ideas unclear.

ANALYTICAL SCORING RUBRIC

CRITERIA FOR EVALUATION	SCORE POINT 4	SCORE POINT 3	SCORE POINT 2	SCORE POINT 1
Conclusion restates the controlling impression and summarizes the points of the description.	Conclusion clearly and freshly restates the controlling impression and concisely summarizes the points of the description.	Conclusion generally restates the controlling impression and summarizes the points of the description.	Controlling impression is missing or conclusion repeats the statement from the introduction; points of the description are missing or simply listed.	Conclusion lacks any restatement of the controlling impression or summary of the points of the description.

Language Conventions

Standard English spelling, punctuation, capitalization, and manuscript form are used appropriately for this grade level.	Standard English spelling, punctuation, capitalization, and manuscript form are used appropriately for this grade level throughout the essay.	Standard English spelling, punctuation, capitalization, and manuscript form are used appropriately for this grade level, with few problems.	Inconsistent use of standard English spelling, punctuation, capitalization, and manuscript form disrupts readers' comprehension.	Minimal use of standard English spelling, punctuation, capitalization, and manuscript form confuses readers.
Standard English sentence and paragraph structure, grammar, usage, and diction are used appropriately for this grade level.	Standard English sentence and paragraph structure, grammar, usage, and diction are used appropriately for this grade level throughout the essay.	Standard English sentence and paragraph structure, grammar, usage, and diction are used appropriately for this grade level, with few problems.	Inconsistent use of standard English sentence and paragraph structure, grammar, usage, and diction disrupts readers' comprehension.	Minimal use of standard English sentence and paragraph structure, grammar, usage, and diction confuses readers.

for **COLLECTION 7** *page 548*

ANALYTICAL SCALE

Speaking: Presenting a Description

Use the chart below to evaluate a descriptive presentation. Circle the numbers that best indicate how well the criteria are met. With these eight criteria, the lowest possible score is 0, the highest 32.

4 = Clearly meets this criterion

3 = Makes a serious effort to meet this criterion and is fairly successful

2 = Makes some effort to meet this criterion but with little success

1 = Does not achieve this criterion

0 = Unscorable

CRITERIA FOR EVALUATION	RATING
Content, Organization and Delivery	
Introduction grabs and holds audience's attention by showing personal involvement with subject.	4 3 2 1
All elements of presentation reinforce controlling impression.	4 3 2 1
Sensory, factual, and figurative details create concrete imagery and convey thoughts and feelings.	4 3 2 1
Conclusion leaves a lasting impression.	4 3 2 1
Organizational pattern is effective.	4 3 2 1
Verbal techniques (enunciation, volume, pace) help the audience understand the subject.	4 3 2 1
Nonverbal techniques (eye contact, gestures, facial expressions) enhance the presentation and are appropriate for the audience and purpose.	4 3 2 1
Language Conventions	
Standard English grammar, usage, and diction are used appropriately for this grade level.	4 3 2 1
Total Points:	

WORKSHOP SCALES AND RUBRICS

ANALYTICAL SCALE

Writing: Short Story

Use the chart below (and the rubric on pages 77–78) to evaluate a short story. Circle the numbers that best indicate how well the criteria are met. With ten criteria, the lowest possible score is 0, the highest 40.

4 = Clearly meets this criterion

3 = Makes a serious effort to meet this criterion and is fairly successful

2 = Makes some effort to meet this criterion but with little success

1 = Does not achieve this criterion

0 = Unscorable

▶ CRITERIA FOR EVALUATION	▶ RATING
▶ **Genre, Organization, and Focus**	
Story begins with exciting event or intriguing introduction to main character.	4 3 2 1
In beginning of story, setting and point of view are established and conflict is introduced.	4 3 2 1
Sensory details and figurative language develop events, characters, and setting.	4 3 2 1
Story contains dialogue.	4 3 2 1
Vivid action verbs are used in story.	4 3 2 1
Conflict is clear, events lead to climax, and all events are relevant to plot.	4 3 2 1
Ending resolves conflict logically.	4 3 2 1
Theme is stated or implied at end of story.	4 3 2 1
▶ **Language Conventions**	
Standard English spelling, punctuation, capitalization, and manuscript form are used appropriately for this grade level.	4 3 2 1
Standard English sentence and paragraph structure, grammar, usage, and diction are used appropriately for this grade level.	4 3 2 1
Total Points:	

ANALYTICAL SCORING RUBRIC

Writing: Short Story

CRITERIA FOR EVALUATION	SCORE POINT 4	SCORE POINT 3	SCORE POINT 2	SCORE POINT 1
Genre, Organization, and Focus				
Story begins with exciting event or intriguing introduction to main character.	Story begins with exciting event or intriguing introduction to main character that grabs readers' attention.	Story begins with interesting event or introduction to main character.	Beginning event or introduction of main character is bland and unexciting.	Beginning does not include event or introduce main character.
In beginning of story, setting and point of view are established and conflict is introduced.	In beginning of story, setting and point of view are firmly established and conflict is clearly presented.	In beginning of story, setting, point of view, and conflict are introduced.	In beginning of story, setting, point of view, or conflict is missing or only vaguely introduced.	In beginning of story, setting, point of view, and conflict are missing or are confusing.
Sensory details and figurative language develop events, characters, and setting.	Abundant sensory details and figurative language create effective images of events, characters, and setting.	Several sensory details and figurative language develop events, characters, and setting, but fall short of creating effective images.	Sparse sensory details and figurative language are not adequate to develop events, characters, and setting.	Sensory details and figurative language are missing.
Story contains dialogue.	Dialogue and interior monologue develop believable characters and reveal their thoughts and feelings.	Dialogue helps characters seem believable.	Little dialogue occurs in story.	Dialogue is missing.
Vivid action verbs are used in story.	Vivid, precise, and powerful action verbs keep story moving.	Vivid action verbs are sprinkled throughout the story.	A few vivid action verbs are used, but most verbs are weak.	Action verbs are consistently weak.
Conflict is clear, events lead to climax, and all events are relevant to plot.	Conflict is clear, events lead from rising action to climax, and all events contribute directly to development of plot.	Conflict is clear, and most events lead to climax, but some events are irrelevant to plot.	Conflict is clear, but events do not develop plot or conflict.	Conflict is never clear, and unrelated events do not develop plot.
Ending resolves conflict logically.	Resolution settles conflict in logical and believable way.	Ending generally resolves conflict, but leaves a few loose ends.	Resolution is largely illogical or unbelievable.	Story just stops, or ending does not resolve conflict and is neither logical nor believable.

WORKSHOP SCALES AND RUBRICS

CRITERIA FOR EVALUATION	SCORE POINT 4	SCORE POINT 3	SCORE POINT 2	SCORE POINT 1
Theme is stated or implied at end of story.	Theme is directly stated or clearly implied and makes significance of story's events clear.	Theme is stated or implied, but its connection to story is not completely clear.	Theme stated or implied does not fit story.	No theme is stated or implied.
Language Conventions				
Standard English spelling, punctuation, capitalization, and manuscript form are used appropriately for this grade level.	Standard English spelling, punctuation, capitalization, and manuscript form are used appropriately for this grade level throughout the essay.	Standard English spelling, punctuation, capitalization, and manuscript form are used appropriately for this grade level, with few problems.	Inconsistent use of spelling, punctuation, capitalization, and manuscript form disrupts readers' comprehension.	Minimal use of spelling, punctuation, capitalization, and manuscript form confuses readers.
Standard English sentence and paragraph structure, grammar, usage, and diction are used appropriately for this grade level.	Standard English sentence and paragraph structure, grammar, usage, and diction are used appropriately for this grade level throughout the essay.	Standard English sentence and paragraph structure, grammar, usage, and diction are used appropriately for this grade level, with few problems.	Inconsistent use of sentence and paragraph structure, grammar, usage, and diction disrupts readers' comprehension.	Minimal use of sentence and paragraph structure, grammar, usage, and diction confuses readers.

WORKSHOP SCALES AND RUBRICS

for **COLLECTION 9** *page 690*   **ANALYTICAL SCALE**

Writing: Research Paper

Use the chart below (and the rubric on pages 80–82) to evaluate a research paper. Circle the numbers that best indicate how well the criteria are met. With twelve criteria, the lowest possible score is 0, the highest 48.

4 = Clearly meets this criterion

3 = Makes a serious effort to meet this criterion and is fairly successful

2 = Makes some effort to meet this criterion but with little success

1 = Does not achieve this criterion

0 = Unscorable

CRITERIA FOR EVALUATION	RATING
Genre, Organization, and Focus	
Attention getter in introduction creates interest in topic.	4 3 2 1
Thesis statement states main idea about the topic and includes main points.	4 3 2 1
Introduction indicates order of main points.	4 3 2 1
Each main point is developed with subpoints in separate body paragraphs.	4 3 2 1
Main points and subpoints are supported with facts and details.	4 3 2 1
Different perspectives found in research are synthesized.	4 3 2 1
Quotations and parenthetical citations are smoothly integrated and document source information.	4 3 2 1
Complex sentences are used to increase sentence variety.	4 3 2 1
Conclusion summarizes main points of research and restates thesis in new way.	4 3 2 1
Paper ends with final insight or dramatic statement.	4 3 2 1
Language Conventions	
Standard English spelling, punctuation, capitalization, and manuscript form are used appropriately for this grade level.	4 3 2 1
Standard English sentence and paragraph structure, grammar, usage, and diction are used appropriately for this grade level.	4 3 2 1
Total Points:	

WORKSHOP SCALES AND RUBRICS

Writing: Research Paper

WORKSHOP SCALES AND RUBRICS

CRITERIA FOR EVALUATION	SCORE POINT 4	SCORE POINT 3	SCORE POINT 2	SCORE POINT 1
Genre, Organization, and Focus				
Attention getter in introduction creates interest in topic.	Compelling attention getter in introduction generates interest in topic for readers.	Attention getter in introduction is fairly interesting.	Attention getter in introduction is bland or unrelated to topic.	There is no attention getter in introduction.
Thesis statement states main idea about the topic and includes main points.	Thesis statement clearly states main idea of paper and includes main points of topic that will be covered.	Thesis statement states main idea of paper but does not suggest all main points.	Thesis statement is incomplete or confusing and unclear.	Introduction omits thesis statement.
Introduction indicates order of main points.	Introduction includes necessary background information and expands on thesis statement by giving clear preview of order main points.	Introduction merely suggests order of main points.	Introduction indicates order of a few main points.	Introduction does not indicate order of main points.
Each main point is developed with subpoints in separate body paragraphs.	Each main point is distinctly developed with subpoints in separate body paragraphs.	Most of the main points are developed in separate body paragraphs.	A few of the main points are developed in separate body paragraphs; some paragraphs include more than one main point.	Main points are all discussed in the same paragraph or are not organized in separate paragraphs.
Main points and subpoints are supported with facts and details.	Each main point and subpoint is supported with evidence—facts and details in the form of direct quotations, paraphrases, and summaries.	Most of the main points are supported with facts and details.	A few of the main points are supported with facts and details.	The main points are largely unsupported by facts or details or any other kind of evidence.

CRITERIA FOR EVALUATION	SCORE POINT 4	SCORE POINT 3	SCORE POINT 2	SCORE POINT 1
Different perspectives found in research are synthesized.	Ways that sources agree or disagree on main points are discussed and synthesized, and interpretations are judged for value and accuracy.	Different perspectives on main points are discussed to some extent.	Different perspectives on main points are mentioned but not discussed.	Different perspectives on main points are not mentioned.
Quotations and parenthetical citations are smoothly integrated and document source information.	Quotations and parenthetical citations documenting source information are appropriately and smoothly integrated within sentences and paragraphs.	Quotations and parenthetical citations are integrated fairly smoothly and document some source information.	Placement of quotations and parenthetical citations is awkward or overdone.	Paper contains no quotations or parenthetical citations.
Complex sentences are used to increase sentence variety.	Complex sentences are used to increase sentence variety and to make ideas flow smoothly.	Many complex sentences are used, along with some short, choppy sentences.	A few complex sentences are used, along with many short, choppy sentences.	The paper is composed almost entirely of short, choppy sentences.
Conclusion summarizes main points of research and restates thesis in new way.	Conclusion clearly and succinctly summarizes main points of research and restates thesis in a fresh, new way.	Conclusion summarizes most main points of research and restates thesis in words different from those in introduction.	Conclusion summarizes a few main points of research and repeats thesis statement from introduction.	Conclusion includes no summary of main points of research and does not contain restatement of thesis.
Paper ends with final insight or dramatic statement.	Paper ends with final insight or dramatic statement that provides a definitive ending and satisfying conclusion clearly related to topic.	Paper ends with final insight or statement that provides a definitive ending related to topic.	Paper ends with final statement that does not bring report to satisfying conclusion.	Paper ends abruptly.

CRITERIA FOR EVALUATION	SCORE POINT 4	SCORE POINT 3	SCORE POINT 2	SCORE POINT 1
Language Conventions				
Standard English spelling, punctuation, capitalization, and manuscript form are used appropriately for this grade level.	Standard English spelling, punctuation, capitalization, and manuscript form are used appropriately for this grade level throughout the essay.	Standard English spelling, punctuation, capitalization, and manuscript form are used appropriately for this grade level, with few problems.	Inconsistent use of spelling, punctuation, capitalization, and manuscript form disrupts readers' comprehension.	Minimal use of spelling, punctuation, capitalization, and manuscript form confuses readers.
Standard English sentence and paragraph structure, grammar, usage, and diction are used appropriately for this grade level.	Standard English sentence and paragraph structure, grammar, usage, and diction are used appropriately for this grade level throughout the essay.	Standard English sentence and paragraph structure, grammar, usage, and diction are used appropriately for this grade level, with few problems.	Inconsistent use of sentence and paragraph structure, grammar, usage, and diction disrupts readers' comprehension.	Minimal use of sentence and paragraph structure, grammar, usage, and diction confuses readers.

Speaking: Presenting Research

Use the chart below to evaluate an oral report of a research paper. Circle the numbers that best indicate how well the criteria are met. With eleven criteria, the lowest possible score is 0, the highest 44.

4 = Clearly meets this criterion

3 = Makes a serious effort to meet this criterion and is fairly successful

2 = Makes some effort to meet this criterion but with little success

1 = Does not achieve this criterion

0 = Unscorable

CRITERIA FOR EVALUATION	RATING
Content, Organization, and Delivery	
Speech begins with attention-getting opening gambit—clever anecdote, wise saying, or sage quotation.	4 3 2 1
Thesis statement states most important main points.	4 3 2 1
One or two main points only are developed in presentation.	4 3 2 1
Important and necessary evidence to support main points is presented.	4 3 2 1
Primary and secondary sources are cited accurately and coherently.	4 3 2 1
Thesis is restated in conclusion.	4 3 2 1
Speech ends with memorable and dramatic turn of phrase.	4 3 2 1
Speech is given extemporaneously, using note cards.	4 3 2 1
Verbal and nonverbal techniques enhance delivery.	4 3 2 1
If used, visuals, graphics, or electronic media supplement presentation of main points.	4 3 2 1
Language Conventions	
Standard English grammar, usage, and diction are used appropriately for this grade level.	4 3 2 1
Total Points:	

ANALYTICAL SCALE

Writing: Comparing a Play and a Film

Use the chart below (and the rubric on pages 85–86) to evaluate an essay comparing a play and a film. Circle the numbers that best indicate how well the criteria are met. With these eleven criteria, the lowest possible score is 0, the highest 44.

4 = Clearly meets this criterion

3 = Makes a serious effort to meet this criterion and is fairly successful

2 = Makes some effort to meet this criterion but with little success

1 = Does not achieve this criterion

0 = Unscorable

CRITERIA FOR EVALUATION	RATING
Genre, Organization, and Focus	
Introduction begins with engaging opener.	4 3 2 1
The original play and playwright and the film adaptation and filmmaker are introduced in first paragraph.	4 3 2 1
Thesis statement identifies the viewer's responses to the film's narrative and film techniques.	4 3 2 1
Film's and play's narrative techniques are compared in point-by-point order.	4 3 2 1
Analysis of film techniques is organized by order of importance.	4 3 2 1
Discussion of each technique is supported with evidence.	4 3 2 1
Sensory details help readers picture scenes that are described.	4 3 2 1
Conclusion restates thesis.	4 3 2 1
Essay ends with closing thought or question.	4 3 2 1
Language Conventions	
Standard English spelling, punctuation, capitalization, and manuscript form are used appropriately for this grade level.	4 3 2 1
Standard English sentence and paragraph structure, grammar, usage, and diction are used appropriately for this grade level.	4 3 2 1
Total Points:	

WORKSHOP SCALES AND RUBRICS

Writing: Comparing a Play and a Film

CRITERIA FOR EVALUATION	SCORE POINT 4	SCORE POINT 3	SCORE POINT 2	SCORE POINT 1
Genre, Organization, and Focus				
Introduction begins with engaging opener.	Introduction begins with engaging opener that grabs readers' attention.	Introduction begins with opener that interests readers.	Introduction begins with a bland statement.	Introduction ignores readers.
The original play and playwright and the film adaptation and filmmaker are introduced in first paragraph.	First paragraph clearly and specifically names the original play and playwright and the film adaptation and filmmaker.	First paragraph names all but one of the original play, playwright, film, and filmmaker.	First paragraph names only one or two of the original play, playwright, film, or filmmaker.	Introduction fails to name play, playwright, film, or filmmaker.
Thesis statement identifies the viewer's responses to the film's narrative and film techniques.	Thesis statement clearly identifies the viewer's emotional and intellectual responses to the film's narrative and film techniques.	Thesis statement is general in identifying the viewer's responses to the film's narrative and film techniques.	Thesis statement vaguely identifies the viewer's responses.	Thesis statement is omitted.
Film's and play's narrative techniques are compared in point-by-point order.	Film's and play's narrative techniques are thoroughly compared in point-by-point order.	Most of film's and play's narrative techniques are compared in point-by-point order.	Film's and play's narrative techniques are listed, but only a few comparisons are made.	Film's and play's narrative techniques are scattered randomly throughout the essay, or only one technique is addressed.
Analysis of film techniques is organized by order of importance.	Analysis of film techniques is clearly organized by order of importance.	Most film techniques are analyzed in order of importance.	Analysis of film techniques does not indicate which technique is most important.	Film techniques are scattered randomly throughout the essay or are omitted.
Discussion of each technique is supported with evidence.	Discussion of each technique is supported with quotations and specific examples from the play or film.	Discussion of most techniques is supported with evidence from the play or film.	Discussion of a few techniques is supported with evidence from either play or film.	Essay contains no evidence from the play or film to support discussion of techniques.
Sensory details help readers picture scenes that are described.	A variety of vivid sensory details helps readers picture scenes that are described.	Sensory details occasionally help readers picture scenes.	Few sensory details are included.	Essay contains no sensory details.

WORKSHOP SCALES AND RUBRICS

CRITERIA FOR EVALUATION	SCORE POINT 4	SCORE POINT 3	SCORE POINT 2	SCORE POINT 1
Conclusion restates thesis.	Conclusion freshly restates thesis in different words.	Conclusion restates thesis in much the same way as in introduction.	Conclusion repeats thesis statement from introduction.	Conclusion contains no restatement of thesis.
Essay ends with closing thought or question.	Essay ends with insightful closing thought or question that gives readers something to consider or ponder.	Essay ends with interesting closing thought or question.	Essay ends with bland closing thought or question.	Essay has no closing thought or question.
Language Conventions				
Standard English spelling, punctuation, capitalization, and manuscript form are used appropriately for this grade level.	Standard English spelling, punctuation, capitalization, and manuscript form are used appropriately for this grade level throughout the essay.	Standard English spelling, punctuation, capitalization, and manuscript form are used appropriately for this grade level, with few problems.	Inconsistent use of spelling, punctuation, capitalization, and manuscript form disrupts readers' comprehension.	Minimal use of spelling, punctuation, capitalization, and manuscript form confuses readers.
Standard English sentence and paragraph structure, grammar, usage, and diction are used appropriately for this grade level.	Standard English sentence and paragraph structure, grammar, usage, and diction are used appropriately for this grade level throughout the essay.	Standard English sentence and paragraph structure, grammar, usage, and diction are used appropriately for this grade level, with few problems.	Inconsistent use of sentence and paragraph structure, grammar, usage, and diction disrupts readers' comprehension.	Minimal use of sentence and paragraph structure, grammar, usage, and diction confuses readers.

WORKSHOP SCALES AND RUBRICS

Listening: Analyzing and Evaluating Speeches

Use the chart below to assess a written evaluation of a historically significant speech. Circle the numbers that best indicate how well the criteria are met. For students who evaluate a recorded speech, use all eleven criteria. With eleven criteria, the lowest possible score is 0, the highest 44. For students who evaluate a written speech, use the first seven criteria and the Language Conventions. With these eight criteria, the lowest possible score is 0, the highest 32.

4 = Clearly meets this criterion

3 = Makes a serious effort to meet this criterion and is fairly successful

2 = Makes some effort to meet this criterion but with little success

1 = Does not achieve this criterion

0 = Unscorable

CRITERIA FOR EVALUATION	RATING
The Student Evaluates	
Arguments (causation, analogy, appeal to authority, emotion, or logic) in speech	4 3 2 1
Kinds of evidence (facts, statistics, examples, and expert testimony)	4 3 2 1
Rhetorical devices and their effect	4 3 2 1
Effect of speaker's language on tone and mood of speech	4 3 2 1
Organizational pattern and clarity of speech	4 3 2 1
Connections of points to each other and to main idea	4 3 2 1
Effectiveness of speech in broadening the view or changing the mind of listener	4 3 2 1
Effectiveness of use of voice	4 3 2 1
Appropriateness and effectiveness of gestures	4 3 2 1
Effect of speaker's delivery on tone and mood of speech	4 3 2 1
Language Conventions	
Standard English grammar, usage, and diction are used appropriately for this grade level.	4 3 2 1
Total Points:	

Writing: Business Letter

Use the chart below to evaluate a business letter. Circle the numbers that best indicate how well the criteria are met. With these seven criteria, the lowest possible score is 0, the highest 28.

4 = Clearly meets this criterion

3 = Makes a serious effort to meet this criterion and is fairly successful

2 = Makes some effort to meet this criterion but with little success

1 = Does not achieve this criterion

0 = Unscorable

CRITERIA FOR EVALUATION	RATING
Genre, Organization, and Focus	
Letter is clear and concise, with no irrelevant details.	4 3 2 1
Style is formal with no slang, contractions, or sentence fragments.	4 3 2 1
Courtesy helps gain reader's cooperation.	4 3 2 1
Tone of letter is formal, yet friendly.	4 3 2 1
Vocabulary takes into account knowledge and interest of reader.	4 3 2 1
Conventional block-style or modified-block-style format is used.	4 3 2 1
Language Conventions	
Standard English is used appropriately for this grade level.	4 3 2 1
Total Points:	

Scales and Sample Papers

Analytical Scale: 6 Traits—Plus 1

IDEAS AND CONTENT

Score 5

The paper is clear, focused, and engaging. Its thoughtful, concrete details capture the reader's attention and flesh out the central theme, main idea, or story line.

- *A score "5" paper has the following characteristics.*

  ✓ The topic is clearly focused and manageable for a paper of its kind; it is not overly broad or scattered.

  ✓ Ideas are original and creative.

  ✓ The writer appears to be working from personal knowledge or experience.

  ✓ Key details are insightful and well considered; they are not obvious, predictable, or humdrum.

  ✓ The development of the topic is thorough and purposeful; the writer anticipates and answers the reader's questions.

  ✓ Supporting details are never superfluous or merely ornamental; every detail contributes to the whole.

Score 3

The writer develops the topic in a general or basic way; although clear, the paper remains routine or broad.

- *A score "3" paper has the following characteristics.*

  ✓ Although the topic may be fuzzy, it is still possible to understand the writer's purpose and to predict how the paper will be developed.

  ✓ Support is present, but somewhat vague and unhelpful in illustrating the key issues or main idea; the writer makes references to his or her own experience or knowledge, but has difficulty moving from general observations to specifics.

  ✓ Ideas are understandable, yet not detailed, elaborated upon, or personalized; the writer's ideas do not reveal any deep comprehension of the topic or of the writing task.

  ✓ The writer does not stray from the topic, but ideas remain general or slightly implicit; more information is necessary to fill in the gaps.

Score 1

The paper does not exhibit any clear purpose or main idea. The reader must use the scattered details to infer a coherent and meaningful message.

- *A score "1" paper has the following characteristics.*

  ✓ The writer seems not to have truly settled on a topic; the essay reads like a series of brainstorming notes or disconnected, random thoughts.

  ✓ The thesis is a vague statement of the topic rather than a main idea about the topic; in addition, there is little or no support or detail.

  ✓ Information is very limited or vague; readers must make inferences to fill in gaps of logic or to identify any progression of ideas.

  ✓ Text may be rambling and repetitious; alternatively, the length may not be adequate for a thoughtful development of ideas.

  ✓ There is no subordination of ideas; every idea seems equally weighted or ideas are not tied to an overarching idea.

Analytical Scale: 6 Traits—Plus 1 *(continued)*

ORGANIZATION

Score 5

Organization enables the clear communication of the central idea or story line. The order of information draws the reader effortlessly through the text.

- A score "5" paper has the following characteristics.

  ✓ The sequencing is logical and effective; ideas and details "fit" where the writer has placed them.
  ✓ The essay contains an interesting or inviting introduction and a satisfying conclusion.
  ✓ The pacing is carefully controlled; the writer slows down to provide explanation or elaboration when appropriate and increases the pace when necessary.
  ✓ Transitions carefully connect ideas and cue the reader to specific relationships between ideas.
  ✓ The choice of organizational structure is appropriate to the writer's purpose and audience.
  ✓ If present, the title sums up the central idea of the paper in a fresh or thoughtful way.

Score 3

Organization is reasonably strong; it enables the reader to move continually forward without undue confusion.

- A score "3" paper has the following characteristics.

  ✓ The essay has an introduction and conclusion. However, the introduction may not be inviting or engaging; the conclusion may not knit all the paper's ideas together with a summary or restatement.
  ✓ Sequencing is logical but predictable. Sometimes, the sequence may be so formulaic that it detracts from the content.
  ✓ At times, the sequence may not consistently support the essay's ideas; the reader may wish to reorder sections mentally or to supply transitions as he or she reads.
  ✓ Pacing is reasonably well done, although sometimes the writer moves ahead too quickly or spends too much time on unimportant details.
  ✓ At times, transitions may be fuzzy, showing unclear connections between ideas.
  ✓ If present, the title may be dull or a simple restatement of the topic or prompt.

Score 1

Writing does not exhibit a sense of purpose or writing strategy. Ideas, details, or events appear to be cobbled together without any internal structure.

- A score "1" paper has the following characteristics.

  ✓ Sequencing needs work; one idea or event does not logically follow another. Organizational problems make it difficult for the reader to understand the main idea.
  ✓ There is no real introduction to guide the reader into the paper; neither is there any real conclusion or attempt to tie things up at the end.
  ✓ Pacing is halting or inconsistent; the writer may slow the pace or speed up at inappropriate times.
  ✓ Ideas are connected with confusing transitions; alternatively, connections are altogether absent.
  ✓ If present, the title does not accurately reflect the content of the essay.

Analytical Scale: 6 Traits—Plus 1 *(continued)*

VOICE

Score 5

The writing is expressive and engaging. In addition, the writer seems to have a clear awareness of audience and purpose.

- *A score "5" paper has the following characteristics.*

  ✓ The tone of the writing is appropriate for the purpose and audience of the paper.

  ✓ The reader is aware of a real person behind the text; if appropriate, the writer takes risks in revealing a personal dimension throughout the piece.

  ✓ If the paper is expository or persuasive, the writer shows a strong connection to the topic and explains why the reader should care about the issue.

  ✓ If the paper is a narrative, the point of view is sincere, interesting, and compelling.

Score 3

The writer is reasonably genuine but does not reveal any excitement or connection with the issue. The resulting paper is pleasant but not truly engaging.

- *A score "3" paper has the following characteristics.*

  ✓ The writer offers obvious generalities instead of personal insights.

  ✓ The writer uses neutral language and a slightly flattened tone.

  ✓ The writer communicates in an earnest and pleasing manner, yet takes no risks. In only a few instances is the reader captivated or moved.

  ✓ Expository or persuasive writing does not reveal a consistent engagement with the topic; there is no attempt to build credibility with the audience.

  ✓ Narrative writing doesn't reveal a fresh or individual perspective.

Score 1

Writing is mechanical or wooden. The writer appears indifferent to the topic and/or the audience.

- *A score "1" paper has the following characteristics.*

  ✓ The writer shows no concern with the audience; the voice may be jarringly inappropriate for the intended reader.

  ✓ The development of the topic is so limited that no identifiable point of view is present; or the writing is so short that it offers little but a general introduction of the topic.

  ✓ The writer seems to speak in a monotone, using a voice that suppresses all excitement about the message.

  ✓ Although the writing may communicate on a functional level, the writing is ordinary and takes no risks; depending on the topic, it may be overly technical or jargonistic.

Analytical Scale: 6 Traits—Plus 1 *(continued)*

WORD CHOICE

Score 5

Words are precise, engaging, and unaffected. They convey the writer's message in an interesting and effective way.

■ *A score "5" paper has the following characteristics.*

✓ All words are specific and appropriate. In all instances, the writer has taken care to choose the right words or phrases.

✓ The paper's language is natural, not overwrought; it never shows a lack of control. Clichés and jargon are rarely used.

✓ The paper contains energetic verbs; precise nouns and modifiers provide clarity.

✓ The writer uses vivid words and phrases, including sensory details; such language creates distinct images in the reader's mind.

Score 3

Despite its lack of flair, the paper's language gets the message across. It is functional and clear.

■ *A score "3" paper has the following characteristics.*

✓ Words are correct and generally adequate, but lack originality or precision.

✓ Familiar words and phrases do not pique the reader's interest or imagination. Lively verbs and phrases perk things up occasionally, but the paper does not consistently sparkle.

✓ There are attempts at engaging or academic language, but they sometimes seem overly showy or pretentious.

✓ The writing contains passive verbs and basic nouns and adjectives, and it lacks precise adverbs.

Score 1

The writer's limited vocabulary impedes communication; he or she seems to struggle for words to convey a clear message.

■ *A score "1" paper has the following characteristics.*

✓ Vague language communicates an imprecise or incomplete message. The reader is left confused or unsure of the writer's purpose.

✓ Words are used incorrectly. In addition, frequent misuse of parts of speech impairs understanding.

✓ Excessive redundancy in the paper is distracting.

✓ The writing overuses jargon or clichés.

Analytical Scale: 6 Traits—Plus 1 *(continued)*

SENTENCE FLUENCY

Score 5

Sentences are thoughtfully constructed, and sentence structure is varied throughout the paper. When read aloud, the writing is fluent and rhythmic.

- *A score "5" paper has the following characteristics.*

    ✓ The sentences are constructed so that meaning is clear to the reader.

    ✓ Sentences vary in length and in structure.

    ✓ Varied sentence beginnings add interest and clarity.

    ✓ The writing has a steady beat; the reader is able to read the text effortlessly, without confusion or stumbling.

    ✓ Dialogue, if used, is natural. Any fragments are used purposefully and contribute to the paper's style.

    ✓ Thoughtful connectives and transitions between sentences reveal how the paper's ideas work together.

Score 3

The text maintains a steady rhythm, but the reader may find it more flat or mechanical than fluent or musical.

- *A score "3" paper has the following characteristics.*

    ✓ Sentences are usually grammatical and unified, but they are routine rather than artful. The writer has not paid a great deal of attention to how the sentences sound.

    ✓ There is some variation in sentence length and structure as well as in sentence beginnings. Not all sentences are constructed exactly the same way.

    ✓ The reader may have to search for transitional words and phrases that show how sentences relate to one another. Sometimes, such context clues are entirely absent when they should be present.

    ✓ Although sections of the paper invite expressive oral reading, the reader may also encounter many stilted or awkward sections.

Score 1

The reader will encounter challenges in reading the choppy or confusing text; meaning may be significantly obscured by the errors in sentence construction.

- *A score "1" paper has the following characteristics.*

    ✓ The sentences do not "hang together." They are run-on, incomplete, monotonous, or awkward.

    ✓ Phrasing often sounds too sing-song, not natural. The paper does not invite expressive oral reading.

    ✓ Nearly all the sentences begin the same way, and they may all follow the same pattern (e.g., subject-verb-object). The result may be a monotonous repetition of sounds.

    ✓ Endless connectives or a complete lack of connectives creates a confused muddle of language.

SCALES AND SAMPLE PAPERS

Analytical Scale: 6 Traits—Plus 1 *(continued)*

CONVENTIONS

Score 5

Standard writing conventions (e.g., spelling, punctuation, capitalization, grammar, usage, and paragraphing) are used correctly and in a way that aids the reader's understanding. Any errors tend to be minor; the piece is nearly ready for publication.

- *A score "5" paper has the following characteristics.*

  ✓ Paragraphing is regular and enhances the organization of the paper.
  ✓ Grammar and usage are correct and add clarity to the text as a whole. Sometimes, the writer may manipulate conventions in a controlled way—especially grammar and spelling—for stylistic effect.
  ✓ Punctuation is accurate; it enables the reader to move through the text with understanding and ease.
  ✓ The writer's understanding of capitalization rules is evident throughout the paper.
  ✓ Most words, even difficult ones, are spelled correctly.

Score 3

The writer exhibits an awareness of a limited set of standard writing conventions and uses them to enhance the paper's readability. Although the writer shows control, at times errors distract the reader or impede communication. Moderate editing is required for publication.

- *A score "3" paper has the following characteristics.*

  ✓ Paragraphs are used, but may begin in the wrong places, or sections that should be separate paragraphs are run together.
  ✓ Conventions may not always be correct. However, problems with grammar and usage are usually not serious enough to distort meaning.
  ✓ Terminal (end-of-sentence) punctuation is usually correct; internal punctuation (e.g., commas, apostrophes, semicolons, parentheses) may be missing or wrong.
  ✓ Common words are usually spelled correctly.
  ✓ Most words are capitalized correctly, but the writer's command of more sophisticated capitalization skills is inconsistent.

Score 1

There are errors in spelling, punctuation, usage and grammar, capitalization, and/or paragraphing that seriously impede the reader's comprehension. Extensive editing is required for publication.

- *A score "1" paper has the following characteristics.*

  ✓ Paragraphing is missing, uneven, or too frequent. Most of the paragraphs do not reinforce or support the organizational structure of the paper.
  ✓ Errors in grammar and usage are very common and distracting; such errors also affect the paper's meaning.
  ✓ Punctuation, including terminal punctuation, is often missing or incorrect.
  ✓ Even common words are frequently misspelled.
  ✓ Capitalization is haphazard or reveals the writer's understanding of only the simplest rules.
  ✓ The paper must be read once just to decode the language and then again to capture the paper's meaning.

PRESENTATION

Score 5

The presentation of the writing is clear and visually appealing. The format helps the reader focus on the message of the writing.

- *A score "5" paper has the following characteristics.*

  ✓ If the paper is handwritten, all letters are formed clearly, and the slant and spacing are consistent.

  ✓ If the paper is word processed, fonts and font sizes are appropriate for the genre of writing and assist the reader's comprehension.

  ✓ White space and text are balanced.

  ✓ Text markers, such as title, headings, and numbering, highlight important information and aid reading of the text.

  ✓ If visuals are used, they are appropriate to the writing, are integrated effectively with the text, and clearly communicate and enhance the message.

Score 3

The presentation of the writing is readable and understandable; however, inconsistencies in format at times detract from the text.

- *A score "3" paper has the following characteristics.*

  ✓ If the paper is handwritten, the handwriting is legible, but some inconsistencies occur in spacing and the formation and slant of letters.

  ✓ If the paper is word processed, fonts and font sizes are inconsistent, sometimes distracting the reader.

  ✓ White space and text are consistent, although a different use of space would make the paper easier to read.

  ✓ Text markers, such as title, headings, and numbering, are used to some degree; however, they are inconsistent and only occasionally helpful to the reader.

  ✓ Visuals are sometimes ineffective and not clearly linked to the text.

Score 1

The presentation and format of the writing are confusing, making the paper difficult to read and understand.

- *A score "1" paper has the following characteristics.*

  ✓ If the paper is handwritten, the letters are formed incorrectly or irregularly. The inconsistent slant and spacing make the paper difficult to read.

  ✓ If the paper is word processed, fonts and font sizes are used randomly or inappropriately, disrupting the reader's comprehension.

  ✓ Spacing appears random, with use of white space either excessive or minimal.

  ✓ Text markers, such as title, headings, and numbering, are not used.

  ✓ Visuals are inaccurate, inappropriate, misleading, or confusing.

Biographical or Autobiographical Narrative Holistic Scale

Score 4	■ *The writing strongly demonstrates*

This distinctly purposeful narrative has an engaging and meaningful introduction, presents a logical sequence of events, and relies on concrete sensory details. The significance of the events is clearly communicated.

- ✓ thorough attention to all parts of the writing task
- ✓ a strong and meaningful purpose, consistent tone and focus, and thoughtfully effective organization
- ✓ a distinct understanding of audience
- ✓ great proficiency in relating a sequence of events and their significance to the audience
- ✓ consistent use of concrete sensory details to describe the sights, sounds, and smells of a scene
- ✓ variation of sentence types using precise, descriptive language
- ✓ a solid command of English-language conventions. Errors, if any, are minor and unobtrusive.

Score 3	■ *The writing generally demonstrates*

This purposeful narrative has a meaningful introduction, presents a logical sequence of events, and clearly communicates the significance of those events.

- ✓ attention to all parts of the writing task
- ✓ clear purpose, a consistent tone and focus, and effective organization
- ✓ an understanding of audience
- ✓ an ability to relate a sequence of events and their significance to the audience
- ✓ frequent use of concrete sensory details to describe the sights, sounds, and smells of a scene
- ✓ variation of sentence types using some descriptive language
- ✓ a command of English-language conventions. Few errors exist, and they do not interfere with the reader's understanding of the narrative.

Score 2	■ *The writing demonstrates*

This narrative has a somewhat vague introduction. The sequence or significance of the events is unclear.

- ✓ attention to only parts of the writing task
- ✓ vague purpose, an inconsistent tone and focus, and less than effective organization
- ✓ little or no understanding of audience
- ✓ a weak ability to relate a sequence of events and their significance to the audience
- ✓ infrequent use of concrete sensory details to describe the sights, sounds, and smells of a scene
- ✓ little variation in sentence type; use of basic, predictable descriptive language
- ✓ inconsistent use of English-language conventions. Errors may interfere with the reader's understanding of the narrative.

SCALES AND SAMPLE PAPERS

Biographical or Autobiographical Narrative Holistic Scale *(continued)*

Score 1

This narrative has a vague introduction and displays no clear purpose. Events are disorganized and their significance is hidden.

- *The writing lacks*

  ✓ attention to most parts of the writing task
  ✓ a purpose (or provides only a weak sense of purpose), a focus, and effective organization
  ✓ an understanding of audience
  ✓ proficiency in relating a sequence of events to the audience
  ✓ concrete sensory details to describe the sights, sounds, and smells of a scene
  ✓ sentence variety and descriptive vocabulary
  ✓ a basic understanding of English-language conventions. Numerous errors often interfere with the reader's understanding of the narrative.

Biographical Narrative: Sample A

PROMPT

Has your understanding of someone you know ever changed? Think of someone you understand better now than when you first met him or her. Then, write a biographical narrative about that person. Be sure to tell why the person is meaningful to you and what happened to change your feelings toward that person. Use concrete sensory details in your narrative.

I'll never forget when I realized there was more to my grandfather than his hard-nosed look and rough exterior. I was about twelve years old during that summer vacation. To me Pa-Paw was a giant with a deep baritone voice and a square, intimidating jaw. Because Pa-Paw did not talk much, I had never felt as if I knew him, but that impression was about to change.

One night, something drew me to the living room, where I saw a side of Pa-Paw I had never seen before. He sat in his favorite chair while the radio next to him wailed country-and-western music. With his blue eyes closed and his gray eyebrows drawn together, Pa-Paw looked ferocious. Then the sad song ended, and a lively tune began. The changes in Pa-Paw made me feel as if I were watching a metamorphosis. His eyebrows eased up. His big feet began tapping on the carpet, and, surprise of all surprises, his mouth lifted into a wide, happy smile. His head came off the back of the chair, and his eyes opened and actually twinkled at me! At that moment, Pa-Paw became a real person to me.

The next day, he surprised me again by asking me to go on his daily walk with him. I was a little nervous but agreed. As we passed under century-old oaks that lined the sidewalk, we didn't speak. Then Pa-Paw began to whistle. That lilting sound reminded me of something I'd long forgotten. "Do you still play the fiddle, Pa-Paw?" I asked, but his mumbled reply was noncommittal.

That night, Pa-Paw didn't turn on the radio. Instead, he went into his bedroom and came out with a fiddle in one hand and a bow in the other. Without saying a word, he

Biographical Narrative: Sample A (continued)

walked stoically out the front door. I looked at Ma-Maw. The wide grin on her face was enough to make me hop up like a jackrabbit and run out onto the darkened porch. Within minutes, Pa-Paw had the fiddle tucked under his jaw and was playing a toe-tapping reel. Seeing him so happy, so filled with music, made me realize he wasn't such a hard man after all. Maybe his tough exterior was just a cover-up.

That's when I started noticing other things—things I'd seen Pa-Paw do a hundred times before but never thought too much about. For example, many times I had watched him feed stray cats. Every night, he'd go out the back door and pour cat food into four or five bowls. I usually paid more attention to the cats, but one night that summer I watched Pa-Paw, too.

"They're cute," I said as he squatted down to pour the food, his broad back rigidly straight.

"They're hungry," Pa-Paw said, his gruff look back in place.

"I think it's nice you feed them," I persisted.

Pa-Paw stood back up, turned, and gave me that hard-nosed look I was so familiar with, but there was something else in that look as well. I smiled. Pa-Paw smiled back. After learning that Pa-Paw's gruff exterior concealed a sensitive, warm man, I wanted to spend every holiday and vacation with Pa-Paw and his cats.

Biographical Narrative: Sample A Evaluation

Holistic Scale

Rating: 4 points

Note: This essay illustrates the type of development appropriate for the prompt, but some teachers may ask their students for longer essays.

Comments: This is an interesting and well-organized biographical narrative. The controlling impression is clear and well supported. Concrete sensory details and well-chosen adjectives help paint a vivid picture of the subject. Sentences are varied in structure and length, and events are presented in a logical sequence. The significance of the events is also clearly related. The narrative shows an excellent command of English-language conventions.

Analytical Scale: 6 Traits—Plus 1

Ratings (High score is 5.)

Ideas and Content: 5	**Sentence Fluency: 5**
Organization: 5	**Conventions: 5**
Voice: 5	**Presentation: 4**
Word Choice: 5	

Comments:

Ideas and Content: The topic is clearly focused and purposeful, showing originality and creativity. The writer is obviously writing from personal experience.

Organization: The introduction is interesting and draws the reader in with a subject to which readers can easily relate. Events are presented effectively and in logical order. Transitions are used effectively to show relationships between ideas.

Voice: A personal dimension is revealed throughout the essay, and the point of view is sincere and compelling.

Word Choice: The writer has taken care to choose words that are specific and appropriate. Concrete sensory details help create distinct images in the reader's mind.

Sentence Fluency: The text flows smoothly and logically. Sentences are varied in length and structure, and they are clear. Dialogue is used naturally and purposefully.

Conventions: Paragraphing is regular and logical. The narrative demonstrates a very strong command of English-language conventions.

Presentation: The presentation is simple and clear.

Biographical Narrative: Sample B

PROMPT

Has your understanding of someone you know ever changed? Think of someone you understand better now than when you first met him or her. Then, write a biographical narrative about that person. Be sure to tell why the person is meaningful to you and what happened to change your feelings toward that person. Use concrete sensory details in your narrative.

I first realized there was more to my grandfather than his mean look during summer vacation when I was about twelve years old. To me Pa-Paw was a giant with a deep voice and a square jaw. Because Pa-Paw didn't talk much I had never felt like I knew him, but that impression was about to change.

One night, I saw a side of Pa-Paw I had never seen before. He sat in his favorite chair while the radio blasted country-and-Western music. Pa-Paw looked sad. Then the sad song ended. A lively tune began. Pa-Paw changed before my eyes; his eyebrows eased up, his big feet began tapping on the carpet, and he smiled. At that moment, Pa-Paw became a real person to me. He surprised me again by asking me to go on his daily walk with him. I was a little nervous but agreed. We didn't speak at first. Pa-Paw began to whistle. That made me think of something. "Do you still play the fiddle, Pa-Paw," I asked, but he just mumbled.

Pa-Paw didn't turn on the radio later. Instead, he got his fiddle out and went out onto the porch. I looked at Ma-Maw. The grin on her face made me hop up and run out onto the porch. Pa-Paw had the fiddle tucked under his chin and was playing a tune. Seeing him so happy made me realize he wasn't such a hard man after all.

I started notising other things. For example, he'd go out the back door and poor cat food in bowls. I usually payed more attention to the cats: one night that summer I watched Pa-Paw.

"They're cute" I said, as he squatted down to poor the food.

"They're hungry" Pa-Paw said, his gruff look back in place.

Biographical Narrative: Sample B *(continued)*

"I think it's nice you feed them" I persisted.

Pa-Paw stood back up, turned, and gave me that look I was so familiar with, but there was something else in that look. Maybe someday I would understand my grandfather better. I smiled. Pa-Paw smiled back.

Biographical Narrative: Sample B Evaluation

Holistic Scale

Rating: 3 points

Comments: This biographical narrative is generally clear and well organized. The controlling impression is clear. Details are provided to help the reader visualize the subject. Tone and focus are consistent. Sentences are varied in structure and length, and events are presented in a logical sequence. The narrative shows a good understanding of English-language conventions, though some misspellings and punctuation errors exist.

Analytical Scale: 6 Traits—Plus 1

Ratings (High score is 5.)

Ideas and Content: 4	**Sentence Fluency: 3**
Organization: 3	**Conventions: 3**
Voice: 4	**Presentation: 4**
Word Choice: 3	

Comments:

Ideas and Content: The topic is clear, but the narrative lacks sufficient vivid descriptions. The writer appears to be writing from personal experience.

Organization: The controlling impression is clearly indicated in the introduction, but it doesn't captivate the reader. The sequence of events is logical, but some necessary transitions are missing.

Voice: The tone is generally appropriate and consistent. The narrative reveals a personal dimension.

Word Choice: Word choice is adequate, but the narrative needs more precise, colorful adjectives in order to make descriptions more vivid.

Sentence Fluency: Sentences are grammatical but routine. Not all sentences begin the same way, but some sections of the narrative are choppy.

Conventions: The writer demonstrates a general command of English-language conventions. Errors in spelling and punctuation stand out but do not impair understanding.

Presentation: The presentation is simple and clear.

SCALES AND SAMPLE PAPERS

STUDENT MODEL

Biographical Narrative: Sample C

PROMPT

    Has your understanding of someone you know ever changed? Think of someone you understand better now than when you first met him or her. Then, write a biographical narrative about that person. Be sure to tell why the person is meaningful to you and what happened to change your feelings toward that person. Use concrete sensory details in your narrative.

    One night when I was about twelve Grandpa sat in his favorite chair while the radio blared country-and-Western music. Pa-Paw looked sad. Then the sad song ended. Then he got happy when a fast song started playing. Once after that he asked me to go on his walk with him. I was a little nervous. We didn't speak at first. Pa-Paw began to whistle. That made me think of something—"Do you still play the fiddle?, Pa-Paw" I asked, but he just mumbled.

    At nighttime he got his fiddle and went out to the porch. I looked at Ma-Maw. She just grinned. Pa-Paw had the fiddle stuck under his chin and was playing a song. He was happy, so then I know he wasn't so mean after all.

    Besides that, I notised other things. He'd go out the back door and poor cat food in bowls. I usually payed more attencion to the cats: one night that summer I watched Pa-Paw. I told him they were cute when he squatted down to poor the food, his back was straight as an arrow.

    "They're hungry" Pa-Paw said, with that mean look again.

    "I think it's nice you feed them" I said. Pa-Paw stood back up and turned, and gave me that same look again, but there was something else in that look too. Someday I might understand grandpa better. I smiled. Pa-Paw smiled back.

Biographical Narrative: Sample C Evaluation

Holistic Scale

Rating: 2 points

Comments: This biographical narrative is poorly organized and vague. No controlling impression is apparent in the introduction. The narrative reads like a list of events, with no logical progression of ideas. Details are few and vague. Sentences are monotonous, choppy, and poorly constructed.

Analytical Scale: 6 Traits—Plus 1

Ratings (High score is 5.)

Ideas and Content: 2	**Sentence Fluency: 2**
Organization: 3	**Conventions: 2**
Voice: 2	**Presentation: 4**
Word Choice: 2	

Comments:

Ideas and Content: A controlling impression can be inferred only after reading the entire narrative. Events are strung together. All ideas seem equally weighted. The narrative is not long enough for a thoughtful development of the ideas.

Organization: There is no real introduction or conclusion. Pacing is inconsistent.

Voice: Because the topic is underdeveloped, an identifiable point of view is unclear. The writing is monotonous and takes few risks.

Word Choice: Vague language leaves the reader confused about the writer's purpose.

Sentence Fluency: Sentences are routine and choppy in places.

Conventions: Serious errors in spelling and punctuation are distracting.

Presentation: The presentation is clear.

Exposition: Holistic Scale

Score 4

This expository writing presents a clear thesis or controlling impression and supports it with precise, relevant evidence.

- *The writing strongly demonstrates*

  ✓ a clear understanding of all parts of the writing task

  ✓ a meaningful thesis or controlling impression, a consistent tone and focus, and a purposeful control of organization

  ✓ use of specific details and examples to support the main ideas

  ✓ a variety of sentence types using precise, descriptive language

  ✓ a clear understanding of audience

  ✓ inclusion of accurate information from all relevant perspectives

  ✓ anticipation of and thorough attention to readers' possible misunderstandings, biases, and expectations

  ✓ a solid command of English-language conventions. Errors, if any, are generally minor and unobtrusive.

Score 3

This expository writing presents a thesis or controlling impression and supports it with evidence.

- *The writing generally demonstrates*

  ✓ an understanding of all parts of the writing task

  ✓ a thesis or controlling impression, a consistent tone and focus, and a control of organization

  ✓ use of details and examples to support the main ideas

  ✓ a variety of sentence types using some descriptive language

  ✓ an understanding of audience

  ✓ inclusion of accurate information from relevant perspectives

  ✓ anticipation of and attention to readers' possible misunderstandings, biases, and expectations

  ✓ an understanding of English-language conventions. Some errors exist, but they do not interfere with the reader's understanding.

Score 2

This expository writing presents a thesis or controlling impression, but the thesis is not sufficiently supported.

- *The writing demonstrates*

  ✓ an understanding of only parts of the writing task

  ✓ a thesis or controlling impression (though not always); an inconsistent tone and focus; and little, if any, control of organization

  ✓ use of limited, if any, details and examples to support the main ideas

  ✓ little variation in sentence types; use of basic, predictable language

  ✓ little or no understanding of audience

  ✓ little or no inclusion of information from relevant perspectives

✓ little, if any, anticipation of and attention to readers' possible misunderstandings, biases, and expectations

✓ inconsistent use of English-language conventions. Several errors exist and may interfere with the reader's understanding.

Score 1

This expository writing may present a thesis or controlling impression, but it is not supported.

- *The writing lacks*

    ✓ an understanding of the writing task, addressing only one part

    ✓ a thesis or controlling impression (or provides only a weak one), a focus, and control of organization

    ✓ details and examples to support ideas

    ✓ sentence variety and adequate vocabulary

    ✓ an understanding of audience

    ✓ accurate information from relevant perspectives

    ✓ anticipation of and attention to readers' possible misunderstandings, biases, and expectations

    ✓ an understanding of English-language conventions. Serious errors interfere with the reader's understanding.

Exposition: Sample A

PROMPT

   Think of a recent news event or new information that you found in more than one kind of media. Then, write an essay comparing how the information is presented by two different media. Remember to anticipate and address readers' possible biases.

Do you want to meet a creature who considered dinosaurs mere morsels for snacking? Recently discovered fossils of a crocodile named Sarcosuchus imperator indicate that this cousin of the modern crocodile may have reached a length of 40 feet and a weight of 18,000 pounds. It isn't every day that paleontologists find evidence of a creature that could treat 20-foot-long dinosaurs as hors d'oeuvres. A comparison of a print magazine version of the story in Science News and Project Exploration's Web site presentation of the story reveals differences in the treatment of the story. The print story provides more scientific information, but the Web site is more entertaining. The differences are related to the expected audience and the limitations of the media in which the story appears.

   The magazine article includes additional information about the discovery of the remains and the basis for the scientists' conclusions about the beast's size and diet. The article's catchy title, "Fossils Indicate . . . Wow, What a Crocodile!" appeals to the reader, but the article itself is a rather straightforward account of the find, with estimates of the size of the creature. Vertebrate paleontologists Paul C. Sereno and Wann Langston are quoted as sources for information about the fossil. The article includes only one photograph, a picture of the fossil skull with the skull of a modern-day adult crocodile shown inside it. The picture caption tells the reader the length of both skulls. The fossil skull is 1.5 meters long, while the modern-day crocodile skull is only 50 centimeters long. The Science News article requires readers' sustained concentration but rewards them with detailed information and sources.

Exposition: Sample A *(continued)*

In contrast, the Project Exploration Web site treats the story as entertainment. The legend at the top of the Web page indicates the intended audience is city kids. Attention-getting techniques include the use of color, with burnt umber framing the page, colored tabs at the top of the page, and a multicolored sidebar along the left margin. There are several links to related sites, and the most entertaining site plays a video about the fossil. Against a swampy background the fossil skull appears, followed by the complete skeleton visible within a huge crocodile, accompanied by the grunting call of a crocodile. In the center of the screen, text about the age of the fossil (110 million years) and the beast's length (40 feet) appears, slowly stretching the full width of the screen to emphasize the magnitude of these numbers. The viewer of the Web site video can almost smell the water-soaked vegetation and stagnant water of the swamp.

The Science News article includes paragraphs of factual information, while the Project Exploration Web site includes little text but lots of eye-catching color and graphics, as well as video and sound. While limited in how they present information, print media usually include large blocks of factual information. The Web site uses the common practice of referring viewers to related Web sites that provide additional information. Though limited by its format, the magazine article is a more authoritative source for a research paper. However, the Web site video gives the viewer a sense of actually visiting SuperCroc and its environment. Print media may provide more information, but Web site videos are more entertaining.

Exposition: Sample A Evaluation

Holistic Scale

Rating: 4 points

Note: This essay illustrates the type of development appropriate for the prompt, but some teachers may ask their students for longer essays.

Comments: This essay presents a clear thesis and supports it with relevant, specific examples. The tone is appropriate, and accurate information is included about the magazine article and the Web site. Readers' potential biases, such as preferring colorful images over in-depth text, are adequately addressed. Sentences are varied and clear, and the writing shows a strong command of English-language conventions.

Analytical Scale: 6 Traits—Plus 1

Ratings (High score is 5.)

Ideas and Content: 5	**Sentence Fluency: 5**
Organization: 4	**Conventions: 5**
Voice: 4	**Presentation: 4**
Word Choice: 4	

Comments:

Ideas and Content: The topic is clearly focused and manageable for this type of paper. The writer seems to be writing from personal experience. The topic is purposeful, information is included from relevant perspectives, and readers' potential biases are addressed.

Organization: The introduction has an interesting opening and a clear—though somewhat delayed—thesis. Main points are logically organized and well supported. The conclusion summarizes main points.

Voice: The tone is appropriate for the purpose and audience. The writing reveals a personal dimension without becoming informal.

Word Choice: The language is natural. Words are specific and appropriate.

Sentence Fluency: A variety of sentence types is used. Sentence construction makes the writing easy to read.

Conventions: The writer demonstrates a strong command of English-language conventions.

Presentation: The presentation is simple and clear.

Exposition: Sample B

PROMPT

Think of a recent news event or new information that you found in more than one kind of media. Then, write an essay comparing how the information is presented by two different media. Remember to anticipate and address readers' possible biases.

Recently discovered fossils of a crocodile named Sarcosuchus imperator indicate that this cousin of the modern crocodile may have reached a length of 40 feet and a weight of 18,000 pounds. A comparison of a print magazine story about the discovery in Science News and Project Explorations's Web site presentation of the discovery reveal differences in the treatment of the story. The print story provides more information but the web site is more entertaining.

The magazine article includes information about the discovery of the remains and the basis for the scientist's conclusions about the beast's size and diet. The articles catchy title, "Fossils Indicate . . . Wow, What a Crocodile!" appeals to the reader, but the article itself is a rather strait-forward account of the find. The Science News article requires readers sustained concentration, but rewards them with detailed information and sources.

The Project Exploration Web site treats the story as entertainment. The legend at the top of the Web Page indicates the intended audience is city kids. There are several links to related sites, and the most entertaining site plays a video about the fossil. The viewer of the Web site video can almost smell the water-soaked vegetation and stagnant water of the swamp.

The Science News article includes paragraphs of factual information, while the Project Exploration Web site includes little text but lots of eye-catching color and graphics, as well as video and sound. While limited in how it presents information, print media usually include large blocks of factual information. The Web site uses the common

Exposition: Sample B *(continued)*

practice of refering viewers to related Web sites that provide additional information. Though limited by its format, the magazine article is a more athoritative source for a research paper. However, the Web site video lets a viewer visit SuperCroc and its environment.

Exposition: Sample B Evaluation

Holistic Scale

Rating: 3 points

Comments: This essay presents a clear thesis. The tone is appropriate, and information is included about the magazine article and Web site. Readers' potential biases are addressed. The essay contains a few errors in punctuation, spelling, and grammar, but they do not interfere with understanding.

Analytical Scale: 6 Traits—Plus 1

Ratings (High score is 5.)

Ideas and Content: 3	**Sentence Fluency: 3**
Organization: 4	**Conventions: 3**
Voice: 3	**Presentation: 4**
Word Choice: 3	

Comments:

Ideas and Content: The thesis is clear, but main points are undeveloped and lack sufficient supporting evidence. The writing makes general rather than specific observations.

Organization: The writing includes a clear thesis, body, and conclusion.

Voice: The tone is appropriate for the audience.

Word Choice: Word choice is simple and clear.

Sentence Fluency: Sentences are varied in length and structure, but few transitions facilitate clarity and flow. The writing is somewhat monotonous.

Conventions: The writing contains careless errors, but they do not interfere with understanding.

Presentation: The presentation is clear.

SCALES AND SAMPLE PAPERS

Exposition: Sample C

PROMPT

Think of a recent news event or new information that you found in more than one kind of media. Then, write an essay comparing how the information is presented by two different media. Remember to anticipate and address readers' possible biases.

Crocodials may have got to be 40 feet long and reached a weight of 18,000 pounds. That according to a recent discovery that has been reported upon. A magazine story about it in *Science News* and *Project Explorations's* Web site presentation of the discovery reveals differences in the way the story was wrote. The print story gives tons more infermation, sometimes even more than you want to read, and the internet site is a whole lot more fun to look at.

The magazine article is loaded with stuff about how the dinosors pieces was found and how the scientist's made up the figurs about its size and food. The article contains lots of words and hardly any pictures—its pretty boring really. You have to reelly con-centrait, but if you can hang in their, youll get lots of news about this creeping beast.

The article has lots of paragraphs loaded with facts, like I said, and the web site gives you lots of colorful graphics, as well as video and sound. Print media usually include large blocks of facts, and so does this one. Lots of web sites are refering view-ers to other Web sites that provide even more information, and so does this one. If you just want a bunch of stuff to put in a research paper, you could use the magazine, but it you want a awesome visit with SuperCroc then you're best bet is definetely to go with the internet.

The Project Exporation Web site treats the story like a video game. The top of the page says "Using the wonders of natural science to inspire city kids," so it must be for kids who play lots of video games. There are links to other sits, and the best one plays a video about the fossil. You can totally almost smell the swamp in them videos. Awesome!

Exposition: Sample C Evaluation

Holistic Scale

Rating: 2 points

Comments: This essay shows a lack of understanding of the writing task. A vague thesis is unsupported by evidence and examples. The tone is inconsistent, sometimes straying into vernacular such as *totally* and *awesome*. Rather than addressing potential reader biases, the essay itself is biased in favor of the Web site. Sentences are strung together with little attention to logical flow and are poorly structured. The writing contains serious errors in grammar, spelling, punctuation, and style.

Analytical Scale: 6 Traits—Plus 1

Ratings (High score is 5.)

Ideas and Content: 2	**Sentence Fluency: 2**
Organization: 2	**Conventions: 1**
Voice: 2	**Presentation: 4**
Word Choice: 2	

Comments:

Ideas and Content: The thesis is vague and unsupported. Information is limited, forcing the reader to make inferences.

Organization: The introduction is uninteresting and vague. Main points are unsupported, and paragraphs lack logical progression.

Voice: The tone is flat and often inappropriate for the audience.

Word Choice: The language is vague and uninspired.

Sentence Fluency: Sentences are monotonous and do not flow logically. Sentences lack variety in structure.

Conventions: Serious errors in grammar, spelling, punctuation, and style are distracting.

Presentation: The presentation is clear.

Response to Literature: Holistic Scale

Score 4

This insightful response to literature presents a thoroughly supported thesis and illustrates a comprehensive grasp of the text and the author's use of literary devices.

- *The writing strongly demonstrates*
  - ✓ a thoughtful, comprehensive understanding of the text
  - ✓ support of the thesis and main ideas with specific textual details and examples that are accurate and coherent
  - ✓ a thorough understanding of the text's ambiguities, nuances, and complexities
  - ✓ a variety of sentence types using precise, descriptive language
  - ✓ a clear understanding of the author's use of literary and stylistic devices
  - ✓ a solid command of English-language conventions. Errors, if any, are generally minor and unobtrusive.

Score 3

This response to literature presents a clear thesis that is supported by details and examples.

- *The writing generally demonstrates*
  - ✓ a comprehensive understanding of the text
  - ✓ support of the thesis and main ideas with general textual details and examples that are accurate and coherent
  - ✓ an understanding of the text's ambiguities, nuances, and complexities
  - ✓ a variety of sentence types using some descriptive language
  - ✓ an understanding of the author's use of literary and stylistic devices
  - ✓ an understanding of English-language conventions. Some errors exist, but they do not interfere with the reader's understanding of the essay.

Score 2

This literary response presents a thesis, but it is not sufficiently supported. The writing shows little understanding of the text.

- *The writing demonstrates*
  - ✓ a limited understanding of the text
  - ✓ little, if any, support of the thesis and main ideas with textual details and examples
  - ✓ limited, or no, understanding of the text's ambiguities, nuances, and complexities
  - ✓ little variety in sentence types; use of basic, predictable language
  - ✓ a limited understanding of the author's use of literary and stylistic devices
  - ✓ inconsistent use of English-language conventions. Several errors exist and may interfere with the reader's understanding of the essay.

SCALES AND SAMPLE PAPERS

Response to Literature: Holistic Scale *(continued)*

Score 1

This literary response contains serious analytical and English-language errors. It shows no understanding of the text or of the author's use of literary devices.

■ *The writing lacks*

✓ a comprehensive understanding of the text
✓ textual details and examples to support the thesis and main ideas
✓ an understanding of the text's ambiguities, nuances, and complexities
✓ sentence variety and adequate vocabulary
✓ an understanding of the author's use of literary and stylistic devices
✓ an understanding of English-language conventions. Serious errors interfere with the reader's understanding of the essay.

Response to Literature: Sample A

> **PROMPT**
>
> Your English class has recently been studying some classic American short stories, such as those by Nathaniel Hawthorne, Edgar Allan Poe, and Ernest Hemingway. Think of a short story you have read, and write an analysis of the story to share with classmates. Remember to focus on the literary and stylistic devices the author uses to set the mood of the story.

For more than 150 years, one writer has thrilled readers with his dark, gloomy tales. In his short story "The Fall of the House of Usher," Edgar Allan Poe uses stylistic devices to establish an ominous setting and foreshadow unhappy events.

From the first sentence of the story, Poe uses diction and imagery to create a sense of foreboding:

> During the whole of a dull, dark, and soundless day in the autumn of the year, when the clouds hung oppressively low in the heavens, I had been passing alone, on horseback, through a singularly dreary tract of country, and at length found myself, as the shades of the evening drew on, within view of the melancholy House of Usher.

Even a reader unfamiliar with Poe's stories is prepared for a sad tale. In the second sentence, the narrator says that "with the first glimpse of the building, a sense of insufferable gloom pervaded my spirit." As the narrator describes the house, he uses personification, a form of figurative language, to intensify the sense of gloom and sadness hanging over the scene. Not only is the house "melancholy," but its windows are "eye-like." Personification of the house itself parallels the story's equation of the house with the Usher family. The grounds in which the house is set also increase the sense of foreboding. On his way to the house, the narrator passes through "a singularly dreary tract of country." The narrator describes his impression upon first viewing the house as "an iciness, a sinking, a sickening of the heart—an unredeemed dreariness of thought." Even viewing the house from a different vantage point does not improve the

Response to Literature: Sample A *(continued)*

narrator's impression of the scene. The first paragraph of the story ends with the narrator viewing "with a shudder even more thrilling than before . . . the ghastly tree-stems, and the vacant and eye-like windows."

As he approaches the house, the narrator sees that "minute fungi overspread the whole exterior, hanging in a fine tangled web-work from the eaves." Almost imperceptible is a narrow crack extending from the roof to the foundation of the house, hinting at a literal interpretation of the story's title. The narrator crosses a causeway and enters the house through a Gothic archway. Inside, somber tapestries hang on the walls, and the floors are black. Poe's emphasis on the gloomy setting prepares the reader for the sad tale of the Usher family. The somberness of the setting is reflected in the history of the family and in recent events affecting Roderick Usher and his twin sister. His twin sister is dying. As the narrator leaves the house, following the deaths of Roderick and his sister, the crack in the house widens and brings the entire house down. Both the deaths and the collapse of the house are foreshadowed by descriptions of the setting.

The narrator's descriptions of the House of Usher from a distance and as he approaches it and his description of the interior of the house establish a sense of foreboding that prepares the reader for the sad plot events. "Vacant and eye-like windows," fungi overspreading the exterior, a narrow crack from roof to foundation, somber tapestries, and black floors all hint at death and decay. His word pictures are more vivid than many paintings.

Response to Literature: Sample A Evaluation

Holistic Scale	Rating: 4 points

Note: This essay illustrates the type of development appropriate for the prompt, but some teachers may ask their students for longer essays.

Comments: This is a thorough, well-written short-story analysis. The analysis shows a thorough understanding of the text's complexities. The thesis is supported by relevant examples, such as the citing of personification used to describe the house. Sentence types are varied and use precise, descriptive language. The writing shows an excellent command of English-language conventions.

Analytical Scale: 6 Traits—Plus 1

Ratings (High score is 5.)

Ideas and Content: 5	**Sentence Fluency: 5**
Organization: 4	**Conventions: 5**
Voice: 4	**Presentation: 4**
Word Choice: 5	

Comments:

Ideas and Content: The thesis is well supported. The writing demonstrates a deep and thoughtful understanding of the text.

Organization: Organization is clear and appropriate. A clear thesis leads to thorough supporting evidence. The conclusion restates the thesis and closes with a logical, thought-provoking comment.

Voice: The tone is appropriate for the audience of students of English.

Word Choice: Precise, appropriate usage shows careful attention to vocabulary.

Sentence Fluency: Sentences are varied and well constructed.

Conventions: The writing shows an excellent command of grammar, usage, and mechanics.

Presentation: The presentation is simple and clear.

Response to Literature: Sample B

STUDENT MODEL

> **PROMPT**
>
> Your English class has recently been studying some classic American short stories, such as those by Nathaniel Hawthorne, Edgar Allan Poe, and Ernest Hemingway. Think of a short story you have read, and write an analysis of the story to share with classmates. Remember to focus on the literary and stylistic devices the author uses to set the mood of the story.

For more than 150 years, one writer has thrilled readers with his scary stories. In his short story, "The Fall of the House of Usher," Edgar Allan Poe uses stylistic devices to establish an ominous setting and foreshadow unhappy events.

From the first sentence of the story, Poe creates a sense of gloom.

> During the whole of a dull, dark, and soundless day in the autumn of the year, when the clouds hung oppressively low in the heavens, I had been passing alone, on horseback, through a singularly dreary tract of country, and at length found myself, as the shades of the evening drew on, within view of the melancholy House of Usher.

Even a reader who doesn't know Poe's stories is prepared for a sad tale. As the narrator describes the house, he uses personefacation to intensify the sense of sadness hanging over the scene. The house is "melancholy" and its windows are "eye-like." Personefacation of the house itself parallels the story's equation of the house with the Usher family. Even viewing the house from a different vantage point does not improve the narrator's impression of the scene.

As he approaches the house, the narrator sees that "minute fungi overspread the whole exterior, hanging in a fine tangled web-work from the eaves." A narrow crack extends from the roof to the foundation of the house, hinting at what might happen. The narrator crosses a causeway and enters the house through an archway. Inside, dull tapestries hang on the walls, and the floors are black. Poe's emphasis on the setting prepares the reader for the sad tale of the Usher family. The somberness of the

Response to Literature: Sample B *(continued)*

setting is reflected in the history of the family and in recent events effecting Roderick and his twin sister who is dying. As the narrator leaves the house following the deaths of Roderick and his sister, the crack in the house widens and the house falls down.

The narrator's descriptions of the house set the scene for the sad story. Poe uses words to create a scary setting so the reader will be prepared for what happens in the house.

SCALES AND SAMPLE PAPERS

Response to Literature: Sample B Evaluation

Holistic Scale

Rating: 3 points

Comments: This analysis has a clear thesis that is supported by general textual details. The writing shows an understanding of the stylistic devices used. Sentence types are varied but lack flair. The writing shows an understanding of English-language fundamentals, though some errors exist in punctuation and spelling.

Analytical Scale: 6 Traits—Plus 1

Ratings (High score is 5.)

Ideas and Content: 3	**Sentence Fluency: 3**
Organization: 4	**Conventions: 3**
Voice: 4	**Presentation: 4**
Word Choice: 3	

Comments:

Ideas and Content: The thesis is well focused, but key points lack adequate support.

Organization: The analysis contains a clear introduction with a well-focused thesis, a clearly organized body, and a conclusion that restates the thesis and summarizes content.

Voice: The tone is appropriate but remains somewhat flat, with neutral language and obvious generalities.

Word Choice: Word choice is correct and free of jargon, but general, commonplace nouns and adjectives could be replaced by more precise, descriptive words.

Sentence Fluency: Sentences are varied in length and grammatically correct, but they are routine rather than artful.

Conventions: The essay contains some errors in punctuation and spelling, but sentences are grammatical.

Presentation: The presentation is clear.

SCALES AND SAMPLE PAPERS

Response to Literature: Sample C

> **PROMPT**
>
> Your English class has recently been studying some classic American short stories, such as those by Nathaniel Hawthorne, Edgar Allan Poe, and Ernest Hemingway. Think of a short story you have read, and write an analysis of the story to share with classmates. Remember to focus on the literary and stylistic devices the author uses to set the mood of the story.

Edgar Poe uses realistic devices to predict unhappy events in his story. From the first sentence of the story, he causes a sense of gloom.

"During the whole of a dull, dark, and soundless day in the autumn of the year, when the clouds hung oppressively low in the heavens, I had been passing alone, on horseback, through a singularly dreary tract of country, and at length found myself, as the shades of the evening drew on, within view of the melancholy house of usher."

Even someone who never read Poe is prepared for something bad to happen. He makes it scary by saying the house is "melancholy" and its windows are "eye-like."

As Edgar walks toward the house he sees a crack running from the roof to the foundation—this is a hint about whats going to happen and also is why it's called the "Fall" of the House of Usher. Ugly tapistrees hang on the walls inside like Spanish Moss from a tree, and the floors are black as coal. The scariness is related to the fact that Roderick's sister is dying. Once she's dead and so is he, the crack in the house gets so big the house falls down like a house of cards.

The scary house gets the reader ready for a sad story. Edgar Allen Poe is one of the best horror story writers ever.

Response to Literature: Sample C Evaluation

Holistic Scale

Rating: 2 points
Comments: This analysis is poorly developed and vague. Although supporting evidence is present, the writing shows little understanding of the text's complexities. Sentences sometimes vary in structure, but very basic, and often incorrect, language is used. Errors exist in grammar, punctuation, capitalization, and usage.

Analytical Scale: 6 Traits—Plus 1

Ratings (High score is 5.)

Ideas and Content: 2   **Sentence Fluency: 2**
Organization: 3   **Conventions: 2**
Voice: 3   **Presentation: 3**
Word Choice: 2

Comments:

Ideas and Content: The malapropism *realistic,* for *stylistic,* causes confusion in the thesis. The thesis can be inferred from evidence in the body of the analysis, but the conclusion shows a lack of understanding.

Organization: The introduction and conclusion are present but show a lack of purpose. The story's title is never properly identified.

Voice: The writing shows an attempt at appealing to an audience of classmates, but the writing is generally flat. Similes used are jarring and inappropriate.

Word Choice: The language is vague and imprecise. Words are used incorrectly, and pronouns are unclear.

Sentence Fluency: Sentences are monotonous and poorly constructed.

Conventions: The analysis contains serious errors in grammar, punctuation, spelling, usage, and capitalization.

Presentation: The presentation is clear.

SCALES AND SAMPLE PAPERS

Persuasion: Holistic Scale

Score 4 This persuasive writing presents a clear position and supports the position with precise, relevant evidence. The reader's concerns, biases, and expectations are addressed convincingly.	■ *The writing strongly demonstrates* ✓ a clear understanding of all parts of the writing task ✓ a meaningful thesis, a consistent tone and focus, and a purposeful control of organization ✓ use of specific details and examples to support the thesis and main ideas ✓ a variety of sentence types using precise, descriptive language ✓ a clear understanding of audience ✓ use of precise, relevant evidence to defend a position with authority, convincingly addressing the reader's concerns, biases, and expectations ✓ a solid command of English-language conventions. Errors, if any, are generally minor and unobtrusive.
Score 3 This persuasive writing presents a position and supports it with evidence. The reader's concerns are addressed.	■ *The writing generally demonstrates* ✓ an understanding of all parts of the writing task ✓ a thesis, a consistent tone and focus, and a control of organization ✓ use of details and examples to support the thesis and main ideas ✓ a variety of sentence types using some descriptive language ✓ an understanding of audience ✓ use of relevant evidence to defend a position, addressing the reader's concerns, biases, and expectations ✓ an understanding of English-language conventions. Some errors exist, but they do not interfere with the reader's understanding of the essay.
Score 2 This persuasive writing presents a position, but the position is not sufficiently supported.	■ *The writing demonstrates* ✓ an understanding of only parts of the writing task ✓ a thesis (though not always); an inconsistent tone and focus; and little, if any, control of organization ✓ use of limited, if any, details and examples to support the thesis and main ideas ✓ little variety in sentence types; use of basic, predictable language ✓ little or no understanding of audience

SCALES AND SAMPLE PAPERS

128 Holt Assessment: Writing, Listening, and Speaking

✓ use of little, if any, evidence to defend a position. The reader's concerns, biases, and expectations are not effectively addressed

✓ inconsistent use of English-language conventions. Several errors exist and may interfere with the reader's understanding of the essay.

Score 1

This persuasive writing may present a position, but it is not supported.

■ *The writing lacks*

✓ an understanding of the writing task, addressing only one part

✓ a thesis (or provides only a weak thesis), a focus, and control of organization

✓ details and examples to support ideas

✓ sentence variety and uses limited vocabulary

✓ an understanding of audience

✓ evidence to defend a position and fails to address the reader's concerns, biases, and expectations

✓ an understanding of English-language conventions. Serious errors interfere with the reader's understanding of the essay.

Persuasion: Sample A

PROMPT

You probably use persuasive arguments all the time without realizing it. Think of an issue that you feel strongly about. Then, write a persuasive essay explaining why readers should agree with you. Be sure to address possible reader biases in your essay.

Shouldn't students have information about as many well-paid careers as possible? Counselors and teachers already provide information about careers that require a college degree, but some career information is missing from our education. We need information about other careers, including those that require on-the-job training.

Competition for jobs is tough, and a college degree does not guarantee a well-paid job. When I stopped at a nursery to take advantage of a sale on houseplants yesterday, I talked with the employee watering the plants. He completed a Ph.D. in mechanical engineering last May, but he is earning little more than minimum wage while he continues to look for a job in his field. He is not the only well-educated individual in such a situation. My neighbor is still looking for a job six months after she was laid off from her job developing software.

Some people have skills and talents that are not developed in traditional high school, college, or university courses. My brother Andre likes to build and repair electronic devices such as TV sets, radios, stereos, and VCRs. He is more interested in working with the actual parts and wiring than in studying in a classroom. My friend Susan enjoys taking apart and rebuilding transmissions. Her father owns the auto repair shop down the street from our school, and Susan has helped in his shop for the past five years. Her father started out teaching her how to change oil and spark plugs, and she enjoyed the work so much that she asked him to teach her how to repair transmissions and car air-conditioning systems. We need introductory courses about careers that require on-the-job training.

Persuasion: Sample A *(continued)*

Most important, though, is the fact that some stable, well-paid careers are not taught in university courses. Mr. Henderson, an electrician who lives across the street from me, usually earns more than $100,000 a year. Even when new construction business is slow, Mr. Henderson finds work rewiring older homes and office buildings. Many people will scrape together the money to pay for electrical or car repairs even when doing so means they must do without entertainment or cultural activities for a while. The failure to provide introductory courses in auto repair, electrical work, and plumbing makes it more difficult for students to learn about these career options.

Not everyone has a father who can train him or her to repair transmissions. Some students do not have access to electronic devices they can use to teach themselves to build or repair the devices. Let's work together to provide information about more career options.

SCALES AND SAMPLE PAPERS

Persuasion: Sample A Evaluation

Holistic Scale	**Rating: 4 points** **Note:** This essay illustrates the type of development appropriate for the prompt, but some teachers may ask their students for longer essays. **Comments:** This persuasive essay is thoroughly developed. The introduction draws the reader in with an attention-getting question. The opinion statement is clear and is amply supported by relevant reasons. Specific evidence provides strong support for the opinion statement and reasons. Possible reader biases, such as a bias for college education and a view that technical careers can be self-taught, are sufficiently addressed. The essay's tone is consistent and appropriate for an audience of high school peers. The writing shows a mastery of English-language conventions.
Analytical Scale: 6 Traits—Plus 1	**Ratings (High score is 5.)**

Ideas and Content: 5   **Sentence Fluency: 4**

Organization: 5   **Conventions: 5**

Voice: 5   **Presentation: 4**

Word Choice: 4

Comments:

Ideas and Content: The subject of the essay is relevant to the audience. The topic is clearly focused, and references to relatives, friends, and neighbors shows that the writer is working from personal knowledge.

Organization: Organization is clear and logical. An interesting introduction leads to several well-supported reasons. The conclusion summarizes the opinion statement and includes a call to action.

Voice: The tone is consistent and appropriate for the audience. A personal dimension helps readers to care about the issue.

Word Choice: Word choice is specific and effective.

Sentence Fluency: Sentences are clear and well constructed.

Conventions: The essay shows careful attention to English-language conventions.

Presentation: The presentation is simple and clear.

Persuasion: Sample B

You probably use persuasive arguments all the time without realizing it. Think of an issue that you feel strongly about. Then, write a persuasive essay explaining why readers should agree with you. Be sure to address possible reader biases in your essay.

Students should have information about as many careers as possible. Counselors and teachers give us information about careers that require a college degree. We need information about other careers, including those that require on-the-job training.

Getting a good job is tough, and a college degree does not guarantee a well-paid job. My neighbor is still looking for a job six months after she was laid off from her job developing software.

Some people have skills and talents that are not developed in traditional high school, college, or university courses. My brother Andre likes to build and repair TV sets, radios, stereos, and VCRs. He is more interested in working with the actual parts and wiring than in studying in a classroom. We need introductory courses about careers that require on-the-job training.

Also, some good careers are not taught in university courses. Mr. Henderson, an electrician who lives across the street from me, usually earns more than $100,000 a year. Many people will scrape together the money to pay for electrical repairs even when it keeps them from enjoying entertainment or cultural activities for a while.

Some students do not have access to electronic devices they can use to teach themselves to build or repair the devices. Let's work together to provide courses that introduce all students to more career options.

SCALES AND SAMPLE PAPERS

Persuasion: Sample B Evaluation

Holistic Scale

Rating: 3 points

Comments: This persuasive essay has a clear opinion statement that is supported by reasons. Possible reader biases are addressed. The essay's tone is consistent and appropriate for an audience of high school peers. The writing shows a mastery of English-language conventions.

Analytical Scale: 6 Traits—Plus 1

Ratings (High score is 5.)

Ideas and Content: 3	**Sentence Fluency:** 3
Organization: 4	**Conventions:** 5
Voice: 3	**Presentation:** 4
Word Choice: 3	

Comments:

Ideas and Content: The opinion statement is clear, but support is underdeveloped. Details and examples do not sufficiently explain reasons or evidence.

Organization: The essay has a clear introduction, reasons, and conclusion. However, the introduction is not engaging, and few transitions connect ideas.

Voice: The tone is flat. Although the writing is clear and pleasing, the reader is seldom captivated or motivated.

Word Choice: Words are correct and accurate but lack precision and originality.

Sentence Fluency: Sentences are varied in length, but sentence structure varies little.

Conventions: The essay shows a strong command of English-language conventions.

Presentation: The presentation is clear.

Persuasion: Sample C

PROMPT

You probably use persuasive arguments all the time without realizing it. Think of an issue that you feel strongly about. Then, write a persuasive essay explaining why readers should agree with you. Be sure to address possible reader biases in your essay.

We should have the scoop about as many jobs as possible even thouth counselors and teachers give us information about careers that require a college degree.

Some people can do lots of things that aren't learned in school; My brother Andre likes to build and repair TV sets, radios, stereos, and VCRs. He likes to be working with the actual parts and wiring lots more than in studying in a classroom. And besides that, we need easier classes about jobs that you learn how to do while you're doing them. Sometimes it can be hard to get a good job, and going to college don't make it a sure bet that your going to get it. My neighbor has been laid off for six months because she made softwair and still didn't get another job

Also, lots of good jobs are not teached about in collages. Mr. Henderson who is a electrition who lives across the street from me usually earns more than one hundred grand every year. He said lots of peeple will scrounge up the green-backs to pay for it when there preshous electrical stuff brakes even when it keeps them from going to there fancy dinners and concerts like the ballet.

Some people dont have all that electric stuff so they can use it to learn about how to build or repair it.

Persuasion: Sample C Evaluation

Holistic Scale

Rating: 2 points

Comments: The opinion statement of this persuasive essay is vague. The tone is inappropriate and inconsistent. The essay is so poorly organized and the opinion statement so vague that it is difficult to distinguish supporting reasons and evidence. The writing shows a very poor understanding of English-language conventions.

Analytical Scale: 6 Traits—Plus 1

Ratings (High score is 5.)

Ideas and Content: 2	**Sentence Fluency: 2**
Organization: 1	**Conventions: 2**
Voice: 2	**Presentation: 4**
Word Choice: 2	

Comments:

Ideas and Content: The opinion statement is vague and unsupported, leaving the reader to fill in gaps by making many inferences.

Organization: The essay has a vague introduction and no real conclusion. Ideas do not progress logically through the essay. Transitions are needed to help the reader make connections between ideas.

Voice: The informal tone is inappropriate for the intended reader, and the topic is underdeveloped.

Word Choice: Vague language communicates a confusing, incomplete message.

Sentence Fluency: The writing includes run-on, monotonous, awkward sentences.

Conventions: Serious errors in grammar, spelling, and punctuation are distracting and impede understanding.

Presentation: The presentation is clear.

Business Letter: Holistic Scale

Score 4

This business letter provides clear, purposeful information. Conventional business-letter style contributes to readability and overall effect. The tone is consistent and appropriate for the intended audience.

- **The writing strongly demonstrates**
  - ✓ a clear understanding of all parts of the writing task
  - ✓ a meaningful message, a consistent tone and focus, and a purposeful control of organization
  - ✓ use of specific details and examples to support the main purpose
  - ✓ a variety of sentence types using precise, descriptive language
  - ✓ a clear understanding of audience
  - ✓ a thorough understanding of conventional business-letter style, with formats, fonts, and spacing that aid readability and have a positive overall effect
  - ✓ a solid command of English-language conventions. Errors, if any, are minor and unobtrusive.

Score 3

This business letter provides clear information. Conventional business-letter style generally contributes to readability. The tone is appropriate for the intended audience.

- **The writing generally demonstrates**
  - ✓ an understanding of all parts of the writing task
  - ✓ a clear message, a consistent tone and focus, and a control of organization
  - ✓ use of details and examples to support the purpose
  - ✓ a variety of sentence types using some descriptive language
  - ✓ an understanding of audience
  - ✓ an understanding of conventional business-letter style, with formats, fonts, and spacing that aid readability and have a positive overall effect
  - ✓ an understanding of English-language conventions. Some errors exist, but they do not interfere with the reader's understanding of the essay.

Score 2

This business letter provides somewhat vague information and strays from its focus. Conventional business-letter style is not used consistently, leaving a negative overall impression.

- **The writing demonstrates**
  - ✓ an understanding of only parts of the writing task
  - ✓ a weak message; an inconsistent tone and focus; and little, if any, control of organization
  - ✓ use of limited, if any, details and examples to support the purpose
  - ✓ little variety in sentence types; use of basic, predictable language
  - ✓ little or no understanding of audience
  - ✓ little understanding of conventional business-letter style. Formats, fonts, and spacing sometimes impede readability.
  - ✓ inconsistent use of English-language conventions. Several errors exist and may interfere with the reader's understanding of the essay.

Business Letter: Holistic Scale (continued)

This business letter shows no understanding of business-letter purpose or style. The tone is inappropriate for the audience. Incorrect style and serious grammatical errors greatly impede readability and have an overall negative effect.

- *The writing lacks*

✓ an understanding of the writing task, addressing only one part

✓ a clear message, a focus, and control of organization

✓ details and examples to support ideas

✓ sentence variety and uses limited vocabulary

✓ an understanding of audience

✓ an understanding of conventional business-letter style. Formats, fonts, and spacing impede readability and have a negative overall effect.

✓ an understanding of English-language conventions. Serious errors interfere with the reader's understanding of the essay.

Business Letter: Sample A

PROMPT

You are interested in working as an intern this summer, and you recently were told about a placement company that helps match qualified high school students with client corporations. Write a business letter to the placement company's human resources department requesting information about the internships. Remember to use both a conventional business-letter format and an appropriate tone.

Vivian Advocatus

830 Morningside Drive

Santa Cruz, CA 95065

March 6, 2003

Human Resources Director

Lotta Jobs Corporation

530 Career Street

Suite 980

Santa Cruz, CA 95060

Dear Sir or Madam:

I am writing to inquire about your summer-internship placement program for high school students. Please send me all relevant information about positions available, prerequisites for the positions, working hours and conditions, and length of the internships.

A friend of my father, Mr. Joe Hatsoff, president and CEO of Tweedcaps Publishing, has worked with interns placed by Lotta Jobs Corp. for the past three summers. Mr. Hatsoff speaks highly of the way Lotta Jobs matches interns with

Business Letter: Sample A *(continued)*

client companies based on both the client's needs and the intern's unique experiences and interests. I am very interested in a law career and am told that you place interns with many area law firms. If possible, please send me specific information about the law firms with which you place summer interns and about their areas of legal specialization.

I truly appreciate your attention to my enquiry and look forward to receiving information on your placement program. Thank you for helping me get a head start in my career.

Sincerely,

Vivian Advocatus

Business Letter: Sample A Evaluation

Holistic Scale

Rating: 4 points

Comments: This business letter is well written and well organized. Correct use of the block-style format makes the letter easy to read and leaves a favorable impression on the reader. The tone is appropriately formal for the audience of a human resources department. Vocabulary is simple and precise, and the letter stays focused on its purpose, requesting information about summer internships for high school students. Sentences are varied and clear, and English-language conventions are strictly observed.

Analytical Scale: 6 Traits—Plus 1

Ratings (High score is 5.)

Ideas and Content: 5	**Sentence Fluency: 4**
Organization: 5	**Conventions: 5**
Voice: 5	**Presentation: 4**
Word Choice: 4	

Comments:

Ideas and Content: The letter is well focused. The writer clearly relates her personal knowledge of Lotta Jobs and her personal interest in a legal career.

Organization: The block-style format is used correctly and is appropriate for the audience. Ideas flow logically, and all elements of a business letter are present and are used appropriately.

Voice: The tone is courteous and consistently formal. The text reveals a personal dimension without becoming informal.

Word Choice: The language is natural while remaining formal throughout. The writer uses simple, direct, and precise wording.

Sentence Fluency: The writing is clear and concise. Sentence beginnings are varied and interesting.

Conventions: The writer demonstrates an excellent command of English-language conventions.

Presentation: The presentation is simple and clear.

SCALES AND SAMPLE PAPERS

Business Letter: Sample B

Vivian Advocatus

830 Morningside Drive

Santa Cruz, CA 95065

March 6, 2003

Human Resources Director

Lotta Jobs Corporation

530 Career Street

Suite 980

Santa Cruz, CA 95060

Dear Sirs:

I am writing to learn more about your placement program for high school students. Please send me all relevant information about the internships that you have available.

A friend of my father's has worked with your interns for the past three summers. He speaks highly of the way Lottajobs matches interns with companies based on both the client's needs and the intern's backgrounds and interests. I am very inter-

SCALES AND SAMPLE PAPERS

Business Letter: Sample B *(continued)*

ested in a law career. I heard that you place interns with many area law firms. If possible, please send me specific information about the law firms that you place summer interns with and about their areas of legal specialisation.

I thank you in advance for your attention to my request, and I really look forward to hearing from you about your placement program. Thank you for helping me get my foot in the door in the career of my dreams.

Sincerely,

Vivian Advocatus

Business Letter: Sample B Evaluation

Holistic Scale

Rating: 3 points

Comments: This business letter is clearly written. With the exception of the salutation, which is incorrectly indented and addresses only "Sirs," block-style format is used correctly and consistently. The tone is generally appropriate for the audience of a human resources department, though the last paragraph is a bit too informal. Vocabulary is simple and clear. English-language conventions are generally observed, though the letter contains some minor errors in spelling and grammar.

Analytical Scale: 6 Traits—Plus 1

Ratings (High score is 5.)

Ideas and Content: 4	**Sentence Fluency: 3**
Organization: 4	**Conventions: 4**
Voice: 3	**Presentation: 4**
Word Choice: 4	

Comments:

Ideas and Content: The letter is clear but includes little background information. The writer relates personal knowledge of the subject.

Organization: With the exception of the salutation, block-style format is used correctly. All elements of a business letter are present.

Voice: The tone is generally appropriate, but in the last paragraph, the phrase "really look forward" and the cliché "get my foot in the door" are too informal.

Word Choice: The language is natural though sometimes too informal. The writer uses simple, direct wording. The salutation should allow for the possibility that either a male or female may receive the letter.

Sentence Fluency: The writing is generally clear, but some sentences are wordy. There is not a lot of variety in sentence structure.

Conventions: The writer demonstrates a good command of English-language conventions. However, the misspelling of the recipient company's name in paragraph two is especially unfortunate.

Presentation: The presentation is simple and clear.

Business Letter: Sample C

PROMPT

You are interested in working as an intern this summer, and you recently were told about a placement company that helps match qualified high school students with client corporations. Write a business letter to the placement company's human resources department requesting information about the internships. Remember to use both a conventional business-letter format and an appropriate tone.

Vivian Advocatus

830 Morningside Drive

Santa Cruz, CA 95065

March 6, 2003

Human Resources Director

Lotta Jobs Corporation

530 Career Street

Suite 980

Santa Cruz, CA

Dear sirs and/or Mrs.,

I'm writing because i'm a highschool scholur and I want to be a adjudicator. Please send me everything you know about the internships that you give to kids who want to be ambitous and get good jobs. My school counselor said you was the place to go for that kind of advice, so that's why I'm writing to you this A.M. I thank you in advance for helping me out in this way. I know wone day I'll look back on this internship as a fantastick leg up, so to speek in my career and might be able to use some of your little interns myself someday.

Most reverently yours,

Vivian Advocatus

Business Letter: Sample C Evaluation

Holistic Scale	**Rating: 2 points**

Comments: This business letter shows that the writer does not understand business-letter format. The format is inconsistent and incomplete, leaving a negative impression. The tone is inconsistent, at times becoming overly formal. The letter contains errors in punctuation, spelling, and grammar.

Analytical Scale: 6 Traits—Plus 1

Ratings (High score is 5.)

Ideas and Content: 2   Sentence Fluency: 2
Organization: 2   Conventions: 2
Voice: 2   Presentation: 2
Word Choice: 2

Comments:

Ideas and Content: The letter is vague and poorly developed. More specific information is needed about the nature of the request.

Organization: The format is a confusing combination of block style and modified block style. The inside address lacks a zip code, and the salutation is incorrect. All information is included in one paragraph. The closing is inappropriately formal.

Voice: The tone is inappropriate for the audience. The letter contains awkward or stilted language ("this A.M." and "Most reverently yours") as well as a colloquial cliché ("fantastick [sic] leg up").

Word Choice: The language is basic, yet the writer has made inappropriate attempts to sound academic, such as using the words *scholur* [sic], *adjudicator,* and *reverently.*

Sentence Fluency: The letter contains rambling sentences that do not flow logically. There is little variety in sentence structure.

Conventions: The writer demonstrates a poor command of English-language conventions. There are errors in spelling, grammar, punctuation, and capitalization.

Presentation: Inconsistencies in format leave an overall negative impression.

Portfolio Assessment

Portfolio Assessment in the Language Arts

Although establishing and using a portfolio assessment system requires a certain amount of time, effort, and understanding, an increasing number of teachers believe that the benefits of implementing such a system richly reward their efforts.

Language arts portfolios are collections of materials that display aspects of students' use of language. They are a means by which students can collect samples of their written work over time so that they and their teachers can ascertain how the students are developing as language users. Because reflection and self-assessment are built-in aspects of language arts portfolios, both also help students develop their critical-thinking and metacognitive abilities.

Each portfolio collection is typically kept in a folder, box, or other container to which items are added on a regular basis. The collection can include a great variety of materials, depending on the design of the portfolio assessment program, the kinds of projects completed inside and outside the classroom, and the interests of individual students. For example, portfolios may contain student stories, essays, sketches, poems, letters, journals, and other original writing, and they may also contain reactions to articles, stories, and other texts the student has read. Other materials that are suitable for inclusion in portfolios are drawings, photographs, audiotapes, and videotapes of students taking part in special activities; clippings and pictures from newspapers and magazines; and notes on favorite authors and on stories and books that the student hopes to read. Many portfolios also include several versions of the same piece of writing, demonstrating how the writing has developed through revision.

Finally, portfolios may contain logs of things the student has read or written, written reflections or assessments of portfolio work, and tables and explanations about the way the portfolio is organized. (A collection of forms that can be used to generate these items may be found at the end of this book.)

The Advantages of Portfolio Assessment

How can portfolio assessment help you meet your instructional goals? Here are some of the most important advantages of using portfolios:

- *Portfolios link instruction and assessment.* Traditional testing is usually one or more steps removed from the process or performance being assessed. However, because portfolio assessment focuses on performance—on students' actual use of language—portfolios are a highly accurate gauge of what students have learned in the classroom.

- *Portfolios involve students in assessing their own language use and abilities.* Portfolio assessment can provide some of the most effective learning opportunities available in your classroom. In fact, the assessment is

Portfolio Assessment in the Language Arts *(continued)*

itself instructional: Students, as self-assessors, identify their own strengths and weaknesses. Furthermore, portfolios are a natural way to develop metacognition in your students. As the collected work is analyzed, the student begins to think critically about how he or she makes meaning while reading, writing, speaking, and listening. For example, the student begins to ask questions while reading, such as "Is this telling me what I need to know?" "Am I enjoying this author as much as I expected to?" "Why or why not?" While writing, the student may ask, "Am I thinking about the goals I set when I was analyzing my portfolio?" That's what good instruction is all about: getting students to use the skills you help them develop.

- ***Portfolios invite attention to important aspects of language.*** Because most portfolios include numerous writing samples, they naturally direct attention to diction, style, main idea or theme, author's purpose, and other aspects of language that are difficult to assess in other ways. The portfolio encourages awareness and appreciation of these aspects of language as they occur in literature and nonfiction as well as in the student's own work.

- ***Portfolios emphasize language use as a process that integrates language behaviors.*** Students who keep and analyze portfolios develop an understanding that reading, writing, speaking, and listening are all aspects of a larger process. They come to see that language behaviors are connected by thinking about and expressing one's own ideas and feelings.

- ***Portfolios make students aware of audience and the need for a writing purpose.*** Students develop audience awareness by regularly analyzing their portfolio writing samples. Evaluation forms prompt them to reflect on whether they have defined and appropriately addressed their audience. Moreover, because portfolios provide or support opportunities for students to work together, peers can often provide feedback about how well a student has addressed an audience in his or her work. Finally, students may be asked to consider particular audiences (parents, classmates, or community groups, for example) who will review their portfolios; they may prepare explanations of the contents for such audiences, and they may select specific papers to present as a special collection to such audiences.

- ***Portfolios provide a vehicle for student interaction and cooperative learning.*** Many projects that normally involve group learning produce material for portfolios. Portfolios, in turn, provide or support many opportunities for students to work together. Students can work as

As they become attuned to audience, students automatically begin to be more focused on whether their work has fulfilled their purpose for writing. They begin to ask questions like, "Did I say what I meant to say? Could I have been clearer and more effective? Do I understand what this writer wants to tell me? Do I agree with it?" Speaking and listening activities can also be evaluated in terms of audience awareness and clarity of purpose.

Portfolio Assessment in the Language Arts *(continued)*

partners or as team members who critique each other's collections. For example, students might work together to prepare, show, and explain portfolios to particular audiences, such as parents, administrators, and other groups interested in educational progress and accountability.

- *Portfolios can incorporate many types of student expression on a variety of topics.* Students should be encouraged to include materials from different subject areas and from outside school, especially materials related to hobbies and other special interests. In this way, students come to see language arts skills as crucial tools for authentic, real-world work.

- *Portfolios provide genuine opportunities to learn about students and their progress as language users.* Portfolio contents can reveal to the teacher a great deal about the student's background and interests with respect to reading, writing, speaking, and listening. Portfolios can also demonstrate the student's development as a language user and reveal areas where he or she needs improvement.

How to Develop and Use Portfolios

As you begin designing a portfolio program for your students, you may wish to read articles and reports that discuss the advantages of portfolio assessment.

Basic Design Features

For a portfolio program to be successful in the classroom, the program should reflect the teacher's particular instructional goals and the students' needs as learners. Teachers are encouraged to customize a portfolio program for their classrooms, although most successful portfolio programs share a core of essential portfolio management techniques. Following are suggestions that teachers will want to consider in customizing a portfolio program.

- *Integrate portfolio assessment into the regular classroom routine.* Teachers should make portfolio work a regular class activity by providing opportunities for students to work with their collections during class time. During these portfolio sessions, the teacher should promote analysis (assessment) that reflects his or her instructional objectives and goals.

- *Link the program to classroom activities.* Student portfolios should contain numerous examples of classroom activities and projects. To ensure that portfolios reflect the scope of students' work, some teachers require that certain papers and assignments be included.

You may want to require that certain papers, projects, and reports be included in the portfolio. Such requirements should be kept to a minimum so that students feel that they can include whatever they consider to be relevant to their language development.

- *Let students have the control.* Students can develop both self-assessment and metacognition skills when they select and arrange portfolio contents themselves. This practice also develops a strong sense of ownership: Students feel that their portfolios belong to them, not to the teacher. When students take ownership of their work, they accept more responsibility for their own language development. To encourage a sense of ownership on the part of students, portfolios should be stored where students can get at them easily, and students should have regular and frequent access to their portfolios.

- *Include students' creative efforts.* To ensure that the portfolios develop a range of language skills, encourage students to include samples of their creative writing, pieces they have written outside class, and publishing activities that they may have participated in, such as the production of a class magazine.

Portfolios that include such planning papers and intermediate drafts are called *working portfolios*. Working portfolios force the student to organize and analyze the material collected, an activity that makes clear to the student that language use is a process.

- *Make sure portfolios record students' writing process.* If portfolios are to teach language use as a process that integrates various language behaviors, they need to contain papers that show how writing grows out of planning and develops through revision. Portfolios should include notes, outlines, clippings, reactions to reading or oral presentations, pictures, and other materials that inspired the final product. Equally vital to the

How to Develop and Use Portfolios *(continued)*

The act of selecting particular papers to show to special audiences—parents, another teacher, or the principal, to name a few—refines students' sense of audience. Preparing and presenting selected collections, called *show portfolios*, engages students in a more sophisticated analysis of their work and encourages them to visualize the audience for the show collection.

If students feel free to include writing and reading done outside class in their portfolios, you can discover interests, opinions, and concerns that can be touched on during conferences. In turn, by communicating interest in and respect for what engages the student, you can promote the success of the portfolio program.

portfolio collections are the different drafts of papers that demonstrate revision over a period of time. Such collections can promote fruitful, concrete discussions between student and teacher about how the student's process shaped the final product.

- *Rely on reactions to reading and listening.* If portfolios are to link and interrelate language behaviors, students must be encouraged to include reactions to things they read and hear. During conferences, teachers may want to point out how some of the student's work has grown out of listening or reading.

- *Encourage students to consider the audience.* Portfolio building prompts students to think about the audience because, as a kind of publication, the portfolio invites a variety of readers. Students will become interested in and sensitive to the reactions of their classmates and their teacher, as well as to the impact of the collections on any other audiences that may be allowed to view them.

- *Promote collaborative products.* Portfolios can promote student collaboration if the program sets aside class time for students to react to one another's work and to work in groups. This interaction can occur informally or in more structured student partnerships or team responses. In addition, many writing projects can be done by teams and small groups, and any common product can be reproduced for all participants' portfolios. Performance projects, speeches, and other oral presentations often require cooperative participation. Audiotapes and videotapes of group projects may be included in portfolios.

- *Let the portfolios reflect a variety of subject areas and interests.* The language arts portfolio should include material from subject areas other than language arts. Broadening the portfolio beyond the language arts classroom is important if the student is to understand that reading, writing, speaking, and listening are authentic activities—that is, that they are central to all real-world activities. Any extensive attempt to limit portfolio contents may suggest to students that these activities are important only in the language arts classroom.

Initial Design Considerations

Using what you have read so far, you can make some initial notes as guidelines for drafting your portfolio assessment design. You can complete a chart like the one on the next page to plan how you will use portfolios and what you can do to make them effective.

How to Develop and Use Portfolios *(continued)*

What are my primary goals in developing my students' ability to use language?	How can portfolios contribute to meeting these goals?	What design features can ensure this?

How to Develop and Use Portfolios *(continued)*

Some key considerations for designing a portfolio program have been suggested. Other considerations will arise as you assess ways to use the portfolios. Here are some questions that will probably arise in the planning stages of portfolio assessment.

How can I introduce students to the concepts of portfolio management?

What examples of student work should go into the portfolios?

What should the criteria be for deciding what will be included?

How and where will the portfolio collections be kept?

Designing a Portfolio Program

How can I introduce students to the concepts of portfolio management?

One way to introduce students to portfolios is to experiment with a group of your students. If you use this limited approach, be sure to select students with varied writing abilities to get a sense of how portfolios work for students with a range of skill levels. To introduce portfolio assessment to them, you can talk to students either individually or as a group about what they will be doing. If other students begin expressing an interest in keeping portfolios, let them take part as well. The kind of excitement that builds around portfolio keeping almost guarantees that some students not included initially will want to get on board for the trial run; some may start keeping portfolios on their own.

You might let students help you design or at least plan some details of the system. After explaining both the reasons for keeping portfolios and the elements of the program that you have decided are essential, you can let students discuss how they think certain aspects should be handled. Even if you decide you want students to make important decisions concerning the program's design, you will need to have a clear idea of what your teaching objectives are and of what you will ask students to do.

What examples of student work should go into the portfolios?

Portfolios should reflect as much as possible the spectrum of your students' language use. What you want to ensure is that student self-assessment leads to the understanding that language skills are essential to all learning. For this to happen, portfolios should contain writing, speaking, and listening activities that relate to a number of subject areas and interests, not just to the language arts. Moreover, the portfolio should include final, completed works as well as drafts, notes, freewriting, and other samples that show the student's thinking and writing process.

FINAL PRODUCTS Students should consider including pieces that are created with a general audience in mind; writing that is communicative and intended for particular audiences; and writing that is very personal and that is used as a method of thinking through situations, evaluating experiences, or musing simply for enjoyment. The portfolios can contain a variety of finished products, including

- original stories, dialogue, and scripts
- poems

How to Develop and Use Portfolios *(continued)*

- essays, themes, sketches
- song lyrics
- original videos
- video or audio recordings of performances
- narrative accounts of experiences
- correspondence with family members and friends
- stream-of-consciousness pieces
- journals of various types

Examples of various types of journals that students might enjoy keeping are described below.

Keeping Journals

A journal is an excellent addition to a portfolio—and one that teachers report is very successful. Journal keeping develops the habit of recording one's observations, feelings, and ideas. At the same time, journal writing is an excellent way to develop fluency. Specifically, it can help tentative writers to overcome the reluctance to put thoughts down as words. Journal keeping can be a bridge over inhibitions to writing and can become a student's favorite example of his or her language use. These benefits support the addition of journals to the portfolio.

Success with journals in encouraging young writers has led teachers to experiment with a variety of types:

PERSONAL JOURNAL This form of journal allows the writer to make frequent entries (regularly or somewhat irregularly) on any topic and for any purpose. This popular and satisfying kind of journal writing develops writing fluency and reveals to students the essential relationship between thinking and writing. (If the journal is kept in the portfolio, you may wish to remind students that you will be viewing it. Tell students to omit anything they would not be comfortable sharing.)

LITERARY JOURNAL OR READER'S LOG This journal provides a way of promoting open-ended and freewheeling responses to student reading. Students are usually allowed to structure and organize these journals in any way that satisfies them. As a collection of written responses, the literary journal is a valuable source of notes for oral and written expression; it can also give students ideas for further reading. Finally, the literary journal is another tool that reveals to students that reading, writing, and thinking are interrelated.

TOPICAL JOURNAL This style of journal is dedicated to a particular interest or topic. It is a valuable experience for students to be allowed to express themselves freely about a specific topic—a favorite hobby, pastime, or issue, for example.

How to Develop and Use Portfolios *(continued)*

As with the literary journal, the topical journal can point students toward project ideas and further reading.

DIALOGUE JOURNAL For this journal format, students select one person—a classmate, friend, family member, or teacher, for example—with whom to have a continuing dialogue. Dialogue journals help develop audience awareness and can promote cooperative learning. If students in your class are keeping dialogue journals with each other, be prepared to help them decide in whose portfolio the journal will go. (Because making copies may be too time consuming or expensive, you could help students arrange alternate custody, or have them experiment by keeping two distinct journals.)

Fragments and Works in Progress

Portfolios should include, in addition to finished products, papers showing how your students are processing ideas as readers, writers, speakers, and listeners. Drafts that show how writing ideas are developed through revision are especially helpful as students assess their work. Items that demonstrate how your language users are working with their collections can include

- articles, news briefs, sketches, or other sources collected and used as the basis for written or oral projects. These sources may include pictures created or collected by students and used for inspiration for the subject.
- reading-response notes that have figured in the planning of a paper and have been incorporated into the final work. Some notes may be intended for future projects.
- other notes, outlines, or evidence of planning for papers written or ready to be drafted
- pieces in which the student is thinking out a problem, considering a topic of interest or behavior, or planning something for the future. These pieces may include pro and con arguments, persuasive points, and reactions to reading.
- freewriting, done either at school or at home
- early versions (drafts) of the latest revision of a piece of writing
- notes analyzing the student's latest draft, which may direct subsequent revision
- solicited reactions from classmates or the teacher
- a published piece accompanied by revised manuscripts showing edits

How to Develop and Use Portfolios *(continued)*

- correspondence from relatives and friends to which students have written a response or to which students need to respond
- journal or diary entries that are equivalent to preliminary notes or drafts of a piece of writing
- tapes of conversations or interviews to which a piece of writing refers or on which it is based

While test results in general do not make good contents for portfolios, performance assessments can provide a focused example of both language processing and integration of reading and writing skills. Such performance tests are now frequently structured as realistic tasks that require reading, synthesizing, and reacting to particular texts. More often than not, these assessments guide the student through planning stages and a preliminary draft. (These parts of the assessment are rarely rated, but they lend themselves directly to self-analysis and should definitely be included with the final draft.)

What should the criteria be for deciding what will be included?

Teachers often want to ensure that students keep certain kinds of papers in the portfolios, while also affirming students' need for a genuine sense of ownership of their collections. Achieving a balance between these two general objectives may not be as difficult as it seems. Students can be informed at the time that they are introduced to the portfolio concept that they will be asked to keep certain items as one part of the overall project. Almost certainly, it will be necessary to explain at some point that the collections are to be working portfolios and that certain records—including many of the forms provided in this booklet—will also need to be included. As they become accustomed to analyzing the papers in their portfolios, students can be encouraged or required to select the contents of their portfolios, using criteria that they develop themselves. Teachers can help students articulate these criteria in informal and formal conferences. Following are criteria teachers or students might consider:

- papers that students think are well done and that therefore represent their best efforts, or papers that were difficult to complete
- subjects that students enjoyed writing about, or texts they have enjoyed reading; things that they think are interesting or will interest others
- things that relate to reading or writing that students intend to do in the future, including ideas that may be developed into persuasive essays, details to support positions on issues, and reactions to favorite literary texts

Discourage the inclusion of workbook sheets, unless they contain ideas for future student writing; they tend to obscure the message that language development is a process, a major component of which is the expression of student ideas and opinions.

You might want to brainstorm a list of things that could be kept in your students' portfolios and then prioritize the items on your list according to which ones you think will be essential for students' development.

PORTFOLIO ASSESSMENT

158 Holt Assessment: Writing, Listening, and Speaking

How to Develop and Use Portfolios *(continued)*

- papers that contain ideas or procedures that students wish to remember
- incomplete essays or projects that presented some problem for the student. He or she may plan to ask a parent, teacher, or fellow student to react to the work or to earlier drafts.
- work that students would like particular viewers of the portfolio (the teacher, their parents, their classmates, and so on) to see, for some reason. This criterion is one that will dictate selections for a show portfolio; it may also determine some of the papers selected for the overall collection.

After building their collections for some time, students should be able to examine them and make lists of their selection criteria in their own words. Doing so should balance out any requirements the teacher has set for inclusion and should ensure students' sense of ownership.

A final note on selection criteria for student portfolios: While portfolios should certainly contain students' best efforts, too often teachers and students elect to collect only their "best stuff." An overemphasis on possible audiences that might view the collection can make it seem important that the collection be a show portfolio. Preparing show portfolios for particular audiences can require students to assess their work in order to decide what is worth including. That is a worthwhile experience, but once the preparation for the show has been completed, student self-assessment ends.

How and where will the portfolio collections be kept?

Part of the fun of keeping portfolios is deciding what the holders for the collections will look like. In a few classrooms, portfolio holders are standardized, but in most classes, the students are allowed to create their own. Many teachers allow students to furnish their own containers or folders, as long as these are big enough to hold the collections without students' having to fold or roll the papers—and not so large as to create storage problems. In addition, many teachers encourage their students to decorate their portfolio holders in unique, colorful, personal, and whimsical ways. Allowing this individuality creates enthusiasm for the project. It also helps students develop a genuine sense of ownership, an important attitude to foster if this system is to succeed.

The kinds of holders that students are likely to bring to school include household cardboard boxes, stationery boxes, folders of various types, paper or plastic shopping bags, computer paper boxes, and plastic and cardboard containers for storing clothing and other items. It would be a good idea to

> Start collecting some samples of holders you can show when you introduce portfolio management to your students. Decorate at least one sample, or have a young friend or relative do it. At the same time, be thinking about areas in your classroom where the collections can be kept.

PORTFOLIO ASSESSMENT

How to Develop and Use Portfolios *(continued)*

have several different examples to show students when discussing how they will keep their papers. It is also a good idea to have some holders on hand for students who are unable to find anything at home that they think is suitable, and for use as replacements for unworkable holders some students may bring, such as shoe boxes that are too small to hold the portfolio items.

The resulting storage area will probably not be neatly uniform but will not necessarily be unattractive, either. Teachers who want a tidier storage area might find similar boxes to pass out to all students, who are then allowed to personalize them in different ways.

The amount of space available in a particular classroom will, of course, determine where students keep their collections, but it is vital that the area be accessible to students. It will save a great deal of inconvenience during the school year if the portfolios are on open shelves or on an accessible ledge of some kind and are not too far from students. If students can retrieve and put away their portfolios in less than a minute or two, there will be many instances when portfolio work can be allowed. Deciding where to keep the portfolios is a decision that may be put off until students know enough about the process to help make the decision.

Open access to portfolios does create the possibility of students looking at classmates' collections without permission and without warning. Remind students not to include in their portfolio anything they would not want others to see. A caution from the teacher could save a student from a wounding embarrassment.

Conferencing with Students

If you are new at conducting portfolio conferences, ask a student who has kept one or more papers to sit down and talk with you. Talk with the student about what he or she thinks is strong about the paper, how it came to be written, and what kind of reading or research the student undertook. See how well you can promote an open-ended conversation related to the topic of the paper and to language use.

The regular informal exchanges between teacher and student about portfolio content are obviously very important, but the more formal conferences that anchor a successful program are of equal if not greater importance. Conferences are evidence that both the teacher and the student take the portfolio collection seriously and that the usefulness of the portfolio depends on an ongoing analysis of it. By blocking out time to conduct at least four formal conferences with each student each year, the teacher demonstrates a commitment to the program and a genuine interest in each student's progress.

Conducting Portfolio Conferences

The conference should proceed as a friendly but clearly directed conversation between the student and the teacher. The focus of the conference should be on how the use of language serves the student's needs and interests. This focus translates, in the course of the conference, into helping each student reflect on why and how he or she reads and writes.

Think about what you could do to ensure a productive portfolio conference that would be helpful and worthwhile to students.

Teachers will want to discuss with students the quantity of recent writing compared with that of previous time periods, the kinds of writing that the student has done, and the student's purposes for writing. Teachers will also want to discuss how the inclusions in the portfolio came to be and whether the pieces represent experiences and ideas the student has enjoyed and thinks are important. Teachers should let students know that the portfolio documents say something important about the individual student's life. In fact, a significant portion of the conference may be dedicated to learning about the student's interests. Here are a few examples of the types of statements that might elicit a helpful response:

- You seem to know a lot about deep-sea diving.
- Where did you learn all those details?
- Have you looked for books about deep-sea diving?
- What kinds of things could you write about deep-sea diving?

The student, too, should feel free to ask questions:

- Which pieces seem the best to the teacher and why?
- Is it always necessary to write for an audience?
- What if I *want* an idea or thought to remain private, though written?
- If I don't know how to spell a certain word, is it OK to just keep writing and look it up later?

PORTFOLIO ASSESSMENT

Conferencing with Students *(continued)*

These examples show how the conference can provide powerful, effective opportunities to teach and to guide language development. The conference conversations between the teacher and the student should be as unique as the individual student who joins the teacher in this exchange.

Ideally, each student will look forward to the conference as a time when student and teacher pay close attention to what the student has done; how the student feels about that performance; and what the student's needs and goals are. Such conferences encourage students to accept responsibility for their own development.

The following guidelines will help the teacher make the most of portfolio conferences.

Conference Guidelines

- *Conferences should be conducted without interruption.* Plan creatively: Perhaps a volunteer assistant can manage the rest of the class during meetings. Or, assign to other students learning activities or other work that does not disrupt your exchange with the student. It may be necessary to conduct the conference outside class time.

- *Keep the focus on the student.* Make the conference as much like an informal conversation as possible by asking questions that will emphasize the student's interests, attitudes toward writing, and favorite topics. Demonstrate that you care about what the student thinks and likes. You can also show that you respect the way a student's individuality is manifested in language use.

- *Let the conversation develop naturally.* Be an active listener: Give full attention to what the student is saying. The student's contribution is likely to suggest a question or comment from you, resulting in a genuine and natural exchange. There may be opportunities to get back to questions you had hoped to ask, but teachers should respect the course that the exchange takes and realize that some of their planned questions will need to be dropped. Good listening on the part of the teacher will help create successful conferences that address individual student interests and needs.

- *Be sincere but not judgmental.* Avoid evaluating or passing judgment on interests or aspects of the student's language use. On the other hand, try to avoid continually expressing approval and thereby creating a situation in which the student tries to respond in a way that will win favor: The conference will then lose its focus on the individual's language needs and development.

For many teachers, the time and planning that the conference demands constitute the most difficult aspect of portfolio assessment. Think about how you can use all the resources at your disposal, and don't forget to enlist students' help. Ask them to help you schedule meetings, and request their cooperation so that the system functions smoothly.

Questions will undoubtedly occur to you while reviewing the student's portfolio. It may be useful to have a few notes to remind you of things you would like to ask. Do not, however, approach a conference with a list that dictates the exchange with the student.

Conferencing with Students *(continued)*

Don't hesitate to use the conference as a means of getting to know the student better by learning about his or her interests, pastimes, concerns, and opinions. This can be time well spent, particularly if it demonstrates to the student that the various aspects of his or her life can be very closely connected to the use and development of language arts skills.

Shortly after the conference, the student can translate his or her notes to a worksheet like the goal-setting form in this book, which will ask the student to elaborate on the objectives that have been established.

- *Keep the conversation open and positive.* It is fine to ask questions that direct the focus back to the collection, as long as that leads in turn to a discussion of ideas and content, the process of writing, and indications of the student's strengths and progress as a language user. In general, however, teachers should ask questions that promise to open up discussion, not shut it down. Phrase questions and comments so that they invite elaboration and explanation.

- *Gear the conference toward goal setting.* Identify and come to an agreement about the goals and objectives the student will be working on during the next time period.

- *Limit the attention devoted to usage errors.* If the student needs to focus on mechanical or grammatical problems, suggest that over the next time period the student pay particular attention to these problems when editing and revising. Do not, however, turn the session into a catalogue of language errors encountered. Keep in mind that if there are four conferences and each one tactfully encourages a focus on just one or two examples of nonstandard mechanical usage, it is possible to eliminate from four to eight high-priority errors during the course of a school year.

- *Keep joint notes with the student on the conference.* To keep a focus on the most important aspects of the conference, you and the student should keep notes. Frequently, student and teacher will record notes based on the same observation: For example, the student might write, "I like to use a lot of verbs at the beginning of my sentences, but maybe I use too many." And the teacher might write, "Let's watch to see how often Cody frontshifts sentence elements for emphasis." The student might write, "Look for a novel about the Civil War." The teacher might note, "Find a copy of *The Killer Angels* for Cody if possible." When the two participants make notes on the same sheet, side by side, the notes on the same point will roughly correspond. The teacher and the student can even write at the same time if they can position the note sheet in a way that will facilitate this.

Keep in mind that conference notes frequently serve as a reference point for an action plan that is then more fully considered on the goal-setting worksheet.

Types of Student-Teacher Conferences

In addition to the scheduled conference, there are several other types of conferences that teachers can conduct as a part of portfolio assessment:

Conferencing with Students *(continued)*

GOAL CLARIFICATION CONFERENCES If a student appears to be having trouble using the portfolio system, a goal clarification conference can be scheduled. The meeting's focus should be to help the student clarify and articulate objectives so that work on the collection is directed and productive.

It is important that this session not be perceived as being overly critical of the student. Be supportive and positive about the collection; try to generate a discussion that will lead to clear goals for the student. These objectives can be articulated on a goal-setting worksheet, which the teacher can help the student fill out.

PUBLICATION STAFF CONFERENCES Students who are publishing pieces they write may frequently meet as teams or in staff conferences to select pieces from their portfolios. They may also discuss possible revisions of manuscripts they hope to publish. Teachers may enjoy observing and even participating in these but should let students direct them as much as possible.

Other class projects and collaborative activities can generate similar student conferences that may involve portfolio collections.

INFORMAL OR ROVING CONFERENCES In these conferences, teachers consult with students about their portfolios during impromptu sessions. For example, at any time a teacher might encounter a student with an important and intriguing question, or spot confusion or a situation developing into frustration for a self-assessor. Often the situation calls for effective questioning and then good listening, just as in the regularly scheduled conferences.

Questions and Answers

The questions that follow are frequently asked by teachers who are thinking about instituting a portfolio management system.

- How can I make my students familiar and comfortable with the idea of creating portfolios?
- How often should my students work on their portfolios?
- How can I keep the portfolios from growing too bulky to manage and analyze effectively?
- Should I grade my students' portfolios?
- Who else, besides the student and me, should be allowed to see the portfolio?
- How can I protect against the possible negative effects of allowing a wide variety of persons to see students' portfolios?

How can I make my students comfortable with portfolios?

Teachers will, of course, want to begin by describing what portfolios are and what they are designed to accomplish. One way to help students visualize portfolios is to point out that some professionals keep portfolios:

- Artists usually keep portfolios to show prospective clients or employers what kind of work they can do. In a sense, an artist's studio is one big working portfolio, full of projects in various stages of completion.
- Photographers, architects, clothing designers, interior designers, and a host of other professionals keep portfolios full of samples of their work.
- Models carry portfolios of pictures showing them in a variety of styles and situations.
- Some writers keep portfolios of their work.
- People who invest their money in stocks and bonds call a collection of different investments a portfolio.

Teachers can encourage students' interest by inviting to the classroom someone who can exhibit and explain a professional portfolio. Teachers might also show students an actual language arts portfolio created by a student in another class or school. Some teachers put together a portfolio of their own and use it as an example for their students.

After this or another introduction, you might share the following information with students:

- Explain what kinds of things will go into the portfolios and why. Students can choose what to include in their collections, but teachers can indicate that a few items will be required, including some records. Without introducing all the records to be used, teachers might show and explain basic forms, such as logs. If forms filled out by students are available, use them as examples.

Questions and Answers *(continued)*

- Stress that portfolios will be examined regularly. If the working portfolios will be available to parents or others, be sure to inform students. If you plan for others to see only show portfolios, this might be a good time to introduce this kind of portfolio.
- Show examples of holders that might be used, and explain where they will be kept. Students can be involved in making decisions about how and where portfolios will be housed.

How often should my students work on their portfolios?

The answer is "regularly and often." Teachers should schedule half-hour sessions weekly; ideally, there will be time almost every day when students can work on their collections. The Scheduling Plan on the next page shows activities that should occur regularly in your program.

How can I keep the portfolios from growing too bulky to manage and analyze effectively?

Because portfolios are intended to demonstrate students' products and processes over time, collections should be culled only when necessary. However, working portfolios can become simply too big, bulky, and clumsy to organize and analyze. If some students find their collections too unwieldy to work with, encourage them to try one of the following techniques:

- Cull older pieces except for those that stand as the best work examples. Put the removed contents into a separate holder and complete an *About This Portfolio* record. Explain on the record that the work consists of less-favored work, and have students take it home for parents to examine and/or save. Photocopies of later work that you consider more successful can be included as comparison.
- Close the whole collection, except for writing not yet completed, notes and records the student intends to use, and other idea files. Send the entire collection home with an explanation record, and start a new portfolio.
- Cull from the collection one or more show portfolios for particular audiences, such as parents, other relatives, other teachers, administrators, or supervisors. After the show portfolio has been viewed, return it to the rest of the collection. Start a new portfolio, beginning with the ideas in progress.

Some teachers have their students prepare a larger decorated box to take home at the beginning of the school year. This container eventually holds banded groups of papers culled during the year. Students then have one repository for their entire portfolio collection, which they can keep indefinitely.

Questions and Answers *(continued)*

▶ SCHEDULING PLAN FOR PORTFOLIO ASSESSMENT

Activity	Frequency	The Student	The Teacher
Keeping logs	As writing and other language experiences are completed; daily if necessary	Makes the entries on the *Writing Record*	Encourages the student to make regular entries and discusses with the student indications of progress, developing interests, etc.
Collecting writing samples, reactions to reading, entries that reflect on oral language	As drafts and reactions to reading become available; can be as often as daily	Selects materials to be included	Can select materials to be included; may require some inclusions
Keeping journal(s)	Ongoing basis; daily to at least once a week	Makes regular entries in one or more journals	Analyzes journal writing discreetly and confidentially
Adding notes, pictures, clippings, and other idea sources	Weekly or more often	Clips and collects ideas and adds them to appropriate place in the portfolio	Reacts to student's idea sources (every month or so); discusses with student how he or she will use them
Explaining, analyzing, evaluating inclusions	Weekly; at least every other week	Uses forms for evaluating and organizing work to analyze and describe individual pieces included	Analyzes inclusions and student analysis of them at least four times a year—before conferences
Completing summary analyses	Monthly and always before conference	Completes a *Summary of Progress* record while comparing it with previously completed summary	Completes selected progress reports at least four times a year—before conferences, relying on student summaries and previously completed records
Conferencing—informal	Ongoing; ideally, at least once a week	Freely asks teacher for advice as often as needed; shares emerging observations with teacher	Makes an effort to observe student working on portfolio at least every two weeks and to discuss one or more specific new inclusions and analyses
Conferencing—formal	At least four times a year	Prepares for conference by completing summaries; discusses portfolio contents and analysis of them with teacher; devises new goals; takes joint notes	Prepares for conference with evaluative analyses; discusses portfolio contents and analysis with student; establishes new goals; takes joint notes
Preparing explanation of portfolio and analysis of it for a particular audience	As occasion for allowing other audiences access arises	Thoughtfully fills out the *About This Portfolio* form	Keeps student advised as to when other audiences might be looking at the student's collection and who the viewer(s) will be
Reacting to a fellow student's paper or portfolio	When it is requested by a "partner" or other classmate	Conferences with peer	Encourages collaboration whenever possible

Questions and Answers *(continued)*

Should I grade my students' portfolios?

Teachers might be tempted to grade portfolios to let students know that they are accountable for their work; teachers may also feel that a grade legitimizes—or at least recognizes—the time and effort that goes into successful portfolio assessment. Finally, many parents, school supervisors, and administrators will expect the teacher to grade the portfolio. These reasons notwithstanding, most portfolio experts recommend that portfolios not be graded. Keep in mind that the collection will contain papers that have been graded. A grade for the collection as a whole, however, risks undermining the goals of portfolio management. Grading portfolios may encourage students to include only their "best" work, and that practice may convey the message that student self-assessment is not taken seriously. Think about it: How would you feel if someone decided to incorporate your journal entries, your collection of ideas that interest you, and other notes and informal jottings into a package that was being rated and given a grade?

Who, besides the student and me, should see the portfolio?

This question raises some of the same concerns as the issue of grading portfolios. Teachers may feel some responsibility to let parents, a supervisor, the principal, and fellow faculty members know how the program is proceeding and what it shows about the progress of individuals or of the class as a whole. It is important to balance the benefits of showing portfolios to outside audiences against the possible adverse effects—the risk of inhibiting students, diminishing their sense of ownership, or invading their privacy. Above all, the primary aims of portfolio assessment must be kept in mind.

Following are some suggestions for showing portfolios, with respect to the audience involved.

Another way to involve parents in portfolio management is to let students plan a workshop on portfolio management geared for parents and others who are interested. Or, as suggested earlier, have students cull their collections periodically and take the materials home for their parents to see.

PARENTS OR GUARDIANS Family members will almost certainly be viewing the portfolio in one form or another. If parents or other responsible adults are to view collections only on more formal occasions, such as back-to-school night or during unscheduled visits to the classroom, then students should be assisted in creating show portfolios. If, on the other hand, the teacher will show students' portfolios without the owners' knowledge or without offering them the opportunity to review the contents beforehand, the teacher must tell students this at the beginning of the year. Warning students of these unscheduled viewings may qualify their sense of ownership; it can also intensify their audience awareness.

Questions and Answers *(continued)*

Again, if portfolios will be shown to other educators, students should be made aware of this before they start to build their collections.

SCHOOL SUPERVISORS AND PRINCIPALS Students' portfolios can demonstrate to fellow educators how youngsters develop as language users, thinkers, and people; they can also show the kind of learning that is taking place in the classroom. When working portfolios are shown, they are usually selected at random from those kept in the class, and the owner's identity is masked. Show portfolios are usually prepared specifically for this purpose. Whether teachers use working or show collections (assuming the state or school system does not mandate one) may depend partly on whether they think the audience will be able to appreciate that the working collections show process.

CLASSMATES Students may review their peers' portfolios as part of the program's assessment. Even if a particular program does not include a formal peer-review stage, remind students that peers may see their collections—either in the process of collaborative work or peer review, or because a student does not respect the privacy of others.

NEXT YEAR'S TEACHERS At the end of the school year, teachers can help students create a show portfolio for their next teacher or teachers. These portfolios should demonstrate the student's growth during the year and the potential of his or her best efforts. They should also indicate the most recent goals established by the teacher and the student, so that the new teacher knows how the student sees his or her language skills developing over the next year.

Encourage students to include finished projects as well as earlier drafts. Discuss what kinds of logs should be included, or have students prepare a brief report showing how goals have been met. A fresh table of contents would be useful, as would an explanation of what the show collection includes and what its purpose is. Teachers may want to let students make copies of some papers that they would also like to take home.

THE STUDENTS THEMSELVES At the end of the school year, portfolio contents can be sent home for parents to see and save, if they wish. Before doing this, teachers may wish to have students prepare a starter portfolio of ideas, writing, plans for reading, and so on, for next year.

How can I protect against the possible negative effects of allowing a wide variety of persons to see students' portfolios?

Whatever special reporting the teacher does with portfolios, he or she needs to offset any possible adverse effects by keeping the primary aims for portfolio assessment in mind.

PORTFOLIO ASSESSMENT

- The overall goal of the program is to develop students as language users. That goal should become the focus of joint student/teacher evaluation of the student's progress.
- Because another important goal is for students to develop a habit of self-assessment, the collections must be readily available to students.
- The emphasis should be on examining the process by looking at the product and the way it is produced. Each portfolio should be a working collection containing notes, drafts, and records of the evaluation of its contents.
- The activities assessed should integrate reading, writing, speaking, and listening.
- The portfolio should be controlled and owned by the student.
- The collections should include reactions to and applications of a variety of text and writing types—with a variety of purposes involving different audiences.

Portfolio Table of Contents

Decide on the major categories for work in your portfolio. Then, in the sections below, list the categories you have chosen. The works themselves may be papers, speech notecards, videotapes, multimedia products, or any work you and your teacher agree should be included. In choosing categories, consider organizing work by topic, by genre (essays, poems, stories, and so on), by chronology (work completed by month, for example), by level of difficulty (work that was less difficult, somewhat difficult, and more difficult), or according to another plan.

Grade: _____ **School year:** _____

▶ WORK IN EACH SECTION	▶ WHY I PUT THIS WORK IN THIS SECTION
Section 1:	
title:	
title:	
title:	
title:	
Section 2:	
title:	
title:	
title:	
Section 3:	
title:	
title:	
title:	

About This Portfolio

Use this form whenever you are preparing your portfolio for review by your teacher or another reader.

Grade: _____ **School year:** _____ **When I began this portfolio:** _____

▶ **How it is organized:**

_____

▶ **What I think it shows about my progress . . .**

as a reader:

_____

as a writer:

_____

as a listener:

_____

as a speaker:

GO ON ➡

About This Portfolio *(continued)*

▶ **Examples of My Best Work**

The best things I have read are—	Why I like them—

The best things I have written are—	Why I like them—

Other things in my portfolio that I hope you notice are— 1. 2. 3.	What they show—

TO PARENT OR GUARDIAN

Home Review: What the Portfolio Shows

In the left-hand column of the chart below, I have noted what I believe this portfolio shows about your child's development in areas such as reading, writing, speaking, and listening. The right-hand column notes where you can look for evidence of that development.

     A prime objective in keeping portfolios is to develop in students a habit of analyzing and evaluating their work. This portfolio includes work that the student has collected over a period of time. The student has decided what to include but has been encouraged to include different types of writing, responses to reading, and evidence of other uses of language. Many of the writings included are accompanied by earlier drafts and plans that show how the work has evolved from a raw idea to a finished piece of writing. The inclusion of drafts is intended to reinforce to the student that using language entails a process of revision and refinement.

▶ I believe that this portfolio shows—	▶ To see evidence of this, please notice—

Teacher's signature_____

PORTFOLIO ASSESSMENT

TO PARENT OR GUARDIAN

Home Response to the Portfolio

▶ Please answer any questions that seem important to you. Use the reverse side for any additional comments or questions.

Parent or Guardian _____ Date _____

What did you learn from the portfolio about your child's reading?

_____

_____

_____

What did you learn from the portfolio about your child's writing?

_____

_____

_____

Were you surprised by anything in the portfolio? Why?

_____

_____

What do you think is the best thing in the portfolio? What do you like about it?

_____

_____

_____

Do you have questions about anything in the portfolio? What would you like to know more about?

_____

_____

_____

What does the portfolio tell you about your child's progress as a writer, reader, and thinker?

_____

_____

_____

Do you think keeping a portfolio has had an effect on your child as a reader or writer—or in another way? If so, what?

_____

_____

_____

Is there anything missing from the portfolio that you would have liked or had expected to see? If so, what?

_____

_____

PORTFOLIO ASSESSMENT

Writing Record

> **Ratings:** ✓✓✓✓ One of my best!   ✓✓ OK, but not my best
>   ✓✓✓ Better if I revise it   ✓ I don't like this one.

Month/ Day	Title and type of writing	Notes about this piece of writing	Rating

PORTFOLIO ASSESSMENT

Spelling Log

▶ Word	▶ My misspelling	▶ How to remember correct spelling

Goal-Setting for Writing, Listening, and Speaking

▶ GOAL	▶ STEPS TO REACH GOAL	▶ REVIEW OF PROGRESS
Writing Goals		

PORTFOLIO ASSESSMENT

GO ON ⟶

Goal-Setting for Writing, Listening, and Speaking *(continued)*

GOAL	STEPS TO REACH GOAL	REVIEW OF PROGRESS
Listening Goals		
Speaking Goals		

Summary of Progress: Writing, Listening, and Speaking

Complete this form before sitting down with your teacher or a classmate to assess your overall progress, set goals, or discuss specific pieces of your work.

Grade : _____ School year: _____ Date of summary: _____

▶ **What work have I done so far this year?**

Writing:

Listening:

Speaking:

▶ **What project do I plan to work on next?**

Writing:

Listening:

Speaking:

▶ **What do I think of my progress?**

What about my work has improved?

What needs to be better?

▶ **Which examples of work are my favorites and why?**

PORTFOLIO ASSESSMENT

SELF-EVALUATION

Summary of Progress: Writing, Listening, and Speaking *(continued)*

▶ **Which pieces of work need more revision, and what is needed?**

▶ **How has listening or speaking helped me in preparing for papers or other projects this year?**

▶ **What a classmate or the teacher thinks about my progress**

In writing—

In listening—

In speaking—

PORTFOLIO ASSESSMENT

Writing Self-Inventory

Questions and answers about my writing	More about my answers
How often do I write?	What types of writing do I do?
Where, besides school, do I write?	What kind of writing do I do there?
Do I like to write?	Why or why not?
Of the things I have written, I like these best:	Why do I like them best?
What topics do I like to write about?	Why do I like to write about these topics?
Is anything about writing difficult for me? What?	Why do I think it is difficult?
Does reading help me to be a better writer or vice versa?	Why do I think this?
How important is learning to write well?	Why do I think this?

Writing Process Self-Evaluation

Choose one paper from your portfolio, preferably one for which you have your prewriting notes and all your drafts. Use the chart below to analyze your writing process. Circle the numbers that most clearly indicate how well you meet the stated criteria in your writing process. The lowest possible total score is 5, the highest, 20.

1 = Do not meet these criteria

2 = Attempt to meet these criteria but need to improve

3 = Are fairly successful in meeting criteria

4 = Clearly meet these criteria

Title of paper _____

▶ STAGE IN WRITING PROCESS	▶ CRITERIA FOR EVALUATION	▶ RATING
Prewriting	■ Use prewriting techniques to find and limit subject and to gather details about subject ■ Organize details in a reasonable way	1 2 3 4
Writing	■ Get most of ideas down on paper in a rough draft	1 2 3 4
Revising	■ Do complete peer- or self-evaluation ■ Find ways to improve content, organization, and style of rough draft ■ Revise by adding, cutting, replacing, and moving material	1 2 3 4
Proofreading	■ Correct errors in spelling, grammar, usage, punctuation, capitalization, and manuscript form	1 2 3 4
Publishing and Reflecting	■ Produce a clean final copy in proper form ■ Share the piece of writing with others ■ Reflect on the writing process and on the paper's strengths and weaknesses	1 2 3 4

Additional Comments:

PORTFOLIO ASSESSMENT

Proofreading Strategies

Proofread your paper using one of the following steps. Put a check by the step you used.

_____ **1.** Read the paper backward word by word.

_____ **2.** Make a large card with a one- or two-inch-sized strip cut into it and read every word in the paper, one at a time, through the hole.

_____ **3.** Read the first sentence in your paper carefully. Put your left index finger on the punctuation mark that signals the end of that sentence. Now, put your right index finger on the punctuation mark that ends the second sentence. Carefully read the material between your fingers; then, move your left index finger to the end of the second sentence and your right to the end of the third sentence, and read carefully. Keep moving your fingers until you have carefully examined each sentence in the paper.

List the mistakes you discovered when proofreading.

_____

_____

_____

_____

_____

_____

_____

_____

_____

_____

_____

_____

_____

Proofreading Checklist

Read through the paper and then mark the following statements either **T** for true or **F** for false. If you are reviewing a classmate's paper, return the paper and checklist to the writer. After the writer has done his or her best to correct the paper, offer to assist if your help is needed.

Writer's name _____ **Title of paper** _____

_____ 1. The paper is neat.

_____ 2. Each sentence begins with a capital letter.

_____ 3. Each sentence ends with a period, question mark, or exclamation mark.

_____ 4. Each sentence is complete. Each has a subject and a predicate and expresses a complete thought.

_____ 5. Run-on sentences are avoided.

_____ 6. A singular verb is used with each singular subject and a plural verb with each plural subject.

_____ 7. Nominative case pronouns such as *I* and *we* are used for subjects; objective case pronouns such as *me* and *us* are used for objects.

_____ 8. Singular pronouns are used to refer to singular nouns, and plural pronouns are used to refer to plural nouns.

_____ 9. Indefinite pronoun references are avoided.

_____ 10. Each word is spelled correctly.

_____ 11. Frequently confused words, such as *lie/lay, sit/set, rise/raise, all ready/already,* and *fewer/less,* are used correctly.

_____ 12. Double negatives are avoided.

_____ 13. All proper nouns and proper adjectives are capitalized.

_____ 14. Word endings such as *–s, –ing,* and *–ed* are included where they should be.

_____ 15. No words have been accidentally left out or accidentally written twice.

_____ 16. Each paragraph is indented.

_____ 17. Apostrophes are used correctly with contractions and possessive nouns.

_____ 18. Commas or pairs of commas are used correctly.

_____ 19. Dialogue is punctuated and capitalized correctly.

_____ 20. Any correction that could not be rewritten or retyped is crossed out with a single line.

Record of Proofreading Corrections

Keeping a record of the kinds of mistakes you make can be helpful. For the next few writing assignments, list the errors you, your teacher, or your peers find in your work. If you faithfully use this kind of record, you'll find it easier to avoid troublesome errors.

Writer's name _____ **Title of paper** _____

Write sentences that contain errors in grammar or usage here.　　　　　　　**Write corrections here.**

_____　　　　_____

_____　　　　_____

_____　　　　_____

_____　　　　_____

_____　　　　_____

_____　　　　_____

_____　　　　_____

Write sentences that contain errors in mechanics here.　　　　　　　**Write corrections here.**

_____　　　　_____

_____　　　　_____

_____　　　　_____

_____　　　　_____

_____　　　　_____

_____　　　　_____

_____　　　　_____

Write misspelled words and corrections here.

_____ _____ _____ _____

_____ _____ _____ _____

_____ _____ _____ _____

_____ _____ _____ _____

_____ _____ _____ _____

Multiple-Assignment Proofreading Record

DIRECTIONS: When your teacher returns a corrected writing assignment, write the title or topic on the appropriate vertical line at right. Under the title or topic, record the number of errors you made in each area. Use this sheet when you proofread your next assignment, taking care to check those areas in which you make frequent mistakes.

TITLE OR TOPIC OF ASSIGNMENT

Type of Error								
Sentence Fragments								
Run-on Sentences								
Subject-Verb Agreement								
Pronoun Agreement								
Incorrect Pronoun Form								
Use of Double Negative								
Comparison of Adjectives and Adverbs								
Confusing Verbs								
Irregular Verbs								
Noun Plurals and Possessives								
Capitalization								
Spelling								
End Punctuation								
Apostrophes								
Confusing Words								
Quotation Marks and Italics								
Comma or Paired Commas								

PORTFOLIO ASSESSMENT

Listening Self-Inventory

▶ Questions and answers about my listening	▶ More about my answers
What kinds of music do I like to listen to?	Why do I like them?
What TV shows and movies are my favorites?	What do I like about them?
How well do I listen in school?	How much do I learn by listening?
Do I listen carefully to what my friends say?	What do I learn from them?
When is it difficult for me to listen?	What makes it difficult?
How do I use the praise and suggestions of others to improve my skills?	How do I feel about getting praise or suggestions for improvement?

Speaking Self-Inventory

▶ Questions and answers about my speaking	▶ More about my answers
How do I feel about speaking to friends?	What do I like to discuss with them?
How do I feel about talking to adults?	Why do I feel this way?
How do I feel about reciting or speaking to the class?	Why do I feel this way?
What is the most difficult thing about speaking?	Why is it difficult?
What techniques have I learned to improve my speaking?	How do I use these techniques with friends or in class?

PORTFOLIO ASSESSMENT

Skills Profile

Student's Name _____ Grade _____

Teacher's Name _____ Date _____

For each skill, write the date the observation is made and any comments that explain the student's development toward skills mastery.

SKILL	NOT OBSERVED	EMERGING	PROFICIENT
Writing			
Writing Modes			
Write an autobiographical narrative.			
Write a biographical narrative.			
Write an essay analyzing problems and solutions.			
Write a persuasive essay.			
Write an essay comparing media genres.			
Write an essay analyzing a short story.			

Skills Profile *(continued)*

SKILL	NOT OBSERVED	EMERGING	PROFICIENT
Write a descriptive essay.			
Write a short story.			
Write a research paper.			
Write an essay comparing a play and a film.			
Write technical documents.			
Write a business letter.			
Writing Process			
Prewriting			
• Choose a topic.			
• Identify purpose and audience.			

Skills Profile *(continued)*

SKILL	► NOT OBSERVED	► EMERGING	► PROFICIENT
• Generate ideas and gather information about the topic.			
• Begin to organize the information.			
• Draft a thesis statement, or a sentence that expresses the main point.			
Writing a Draft			
• State the main points and include relevant support and elaboration.			
• Follow a plan of organization.			
Revising			
• Revise for content and style.			
Publishing			
• Proofread for grammar, usage, and mechanics.			

Skills Profile *(continued)*

SKILL	NOT OBSERVED	EMERGING	PROFICIENT
• Publish the work, or share the finished writing with readers.			
• Reflect on the writing experience.			
Listening and Speaking			
Present an autobiographical narrative.			
Deliver a persuasive speech.			
Participate in a debate.			
Present an oral response to literature.			
Give an oral presentation of a descriptive essay.			

Skills Profile *(continued)*

SKILL	NOT OBSERVED	EMERGING	PROFICIENT
Present a research report.			
Analyze and evaluate speeches.			
Plan and organize the speech or presentation.			
Rehearse and deliver the presentation.			
Use effective verbal and nonverbal techniques.			
Analyze content, organization, and delivery.			